Workshop on Information Extraction Beyond the Document 2006

Held in conjunction with COLING/ACL 2006

Sydney, Australia
22 July 2006

ISBN: 978-1-61738-501-8

Printed from e-media with permission by:

Curran Associates, Inc.
57 Morehouse Lane
Red Hook, NY 12571
www.proceedings.com

Some format issues inherent in the e-media version may also appear in this print version.

Printed by Curran Associates, Inc. (2010)

Association for Computational Linguistics
209 N. Eighth Street
Stroudsburg, Pennsylvania 18360

Phone: 1-570-476-8006
Fax: 1-570-476-0860

acl@aclweb.org

Table of Contents

Preface

Traditional approaches to the development and evaluation of Information Extraction (IE) systems have relied on relatively small collections of up to a few hundred documents tagged with detailed semantic annotations. While this paradigm has enabled rapid advances in IE technology, it remains constrained by a dependence on annotated documents and does not make use of the information available in large corpora. Alternative approaches, which make use of large text collections and inter-document information, are now beginning to emerge – as evidenced by a parallel emergence of interest in learning from unlabelled data in AI in general. For example, some systems learn extraction patterns by exploiting information about their distribution across corpora; others exploit the redundancy of the Internet by assuming that facts with multiple mentions are more reliable. These approaches require large amounts of unannotated text, which is generally easy to obtain, and employ unsupervised or minimally supervised learning algorithms, as well as related techniques such as co-training and active learning. These alternative approaches are complementary to the established IE paradigm based on supervised training, and are now forming a cohesive emergent trend in recent research. They constitute the focus of this workshop.

There are several advantages to employing large text collections for IE. They provide enormous amounts of training data, albeit mostly unannotated. Facts can be extracted from, or verified across, multiple documents. Large text collections often contain vast amounts of redundancy in the form of multiple references to or mentions of closely related facts. Redundancy can be exploited in the IE setting to identify trends and patterns within the text, e.g., by means of Data Mining techniques.

For this workshop, we solicited papers presenting new, original work on learning extraction rules or identifying facts across document boundaries while exploiting sizable amounts of unlabelled text in the training stage, in the extraction stage, or both.

Eight papers were selected for inclusion in the workshop following a peer reviewing process. These papers cover a wide range of topics in Information Extraction including traditional IE tasks such as name tagging and relation extraction as well as other topics which are relevant to IE such as terminology extraction, trend identification and lexical chains. The papers describe a number of techniques including using the web as a data source and semi-supervised machine learning. We hope these will form the basis of a productive workshop, and will stimulate further research into this area, which we believe is worth pursuing.

Mary Elaine Califf
Mark A. Greenwood
Mark Stevenson
Roman Yangarber

Organizers

Chairs:

Mary Elaine Califf, Illinois State University
Mark A. Greenwood, University of Sheffield
Mark Stevenson, University of Sheffield
Roman Yangarber, University of Helsinki

Program Committee:

Markus Ackermann, University of Leipzig
Amit Bagga, AskJeeves
Roberto Basili, University of Rome, Tor Vergata
Antal van den Bosch, Tilburg University
Neus Catala, Universitat Politècnica de Catalunya
Walter Daelemans, University of Antwerp
Jenny Rose Finkel, Stanford University
Robert Gaizauskas, University of Sheffield
Ralph Grishman, New York University
Takaaki Hasegawa, NTT
Heng Ji, New York University
Nick Kushmerick, University College Dublin
Alberto Lavelli, ITC-IRST
Gideon Mann, John Hopkin's University
Ion Muslea, Language Weaver Inc.
Chikashi Nobata, Sharp
Ellen Riloff, University of Utah
Stephen Soderland, University of Washington
Yorick Wilks, University of Sheffield

Workshop Program

Saturday, 22 July 2006

9:10–9:20 Welcome

9:20–9:55 *Development of an Automatic Trend Exploration System using the MuST Data Collection*
Masaki Murata, Koji Ichii, Qing Ma, Tamotsu Shirado, Toshiyuki Kanamaru, Sachiyo Tsukawaki and Hitoshi Isahara

9:55–10:30 *Comparing Information Extraction Pattern Models*
Mark Stevenson and Mark A. Greenwood

10:30–11:00 Coffee Break

11:00–11:35 *Automatic Extraction of Definitions from German Court Decisions*
Stephan Walter and Manfred Pinkal

11:35–12:10 *Improving Semi-supervised Acquisition of Relation Extraction Patterns*
Mark A. Greenwood and Mark Stevenson

12:10–13:45 Lunch

13:45–14:20 *Automatic Knowledge Representation using a Graph-based Algorithm for Language-Independent Lexical Chaining*
Gaël Dias, Cláudia Santos and Guillaume Cleuziou

14:20–14:55 *Data Selection in Semi-supervised Learning for Name Tagging*
Heng Ji and Ralph Grishman

14:55–15:30 *LoLo: A System based on Terminology for Multilingual Extraction*
Yousif Almas and Khurshid Ahmad

15:30–16:00 Coffee Break

16:00–16:35 *Learning Domain-Specific Information Extraction Patterns from the Web*
Siddharth Patwardhan and Ellen Riloff

16:35–17:00 Discussion

Development of an automatic trend exploration system using the MuST data collection

Masaki Murata[1]
murata@nict.go.jp

Koji Ichii[2]
ichiikoji@hiroshima-u.ac.jp

Qing Ma[3,1]
[3]qma@math.ryukoku.ac.jp

Tamotsu Shirado[1]
shirado@nict.go.jp

Toshiyuki Kanamaru[1,4]
[1]kanamaru@nict.go.jp

Sachiyo Tsukawaki[1]
tsuka@nict.go.jp

Hitoshi Isahara[1]
isahara@nict.go.jp

[1]National Institute of Information and Communications Technology
3-5 Hikaridai, Seika-cho, Soraku-gun, Kyoto 619-0289, Japan

[2]Hiroshima University
1-4-1 Kagamiyama, Higashi-hiroshima, Hiroshima 739-8527, Japan

[3]Ryukoku University
Otsu, Shiga, 520-2194, Japan

[4]Kyoto University
Yoshida-nihonmatsu-cho, Sakyo-ku, Kyoto, 606-8501, Japan

Abstract

The automatic extraction of trend information from text documents such as newspaper articles would be useful for exploring and examining trends. To enable this, we used data sets provided by a workshop on multimodal summarization for trend information (the MuST Workshop) to construct an automatic trend exploration system. This system first extracts units, temporals, and item expressions from newspaper articles, then it extracts sets of expressions as trend information, and finally it arranges the sets and displays them in graphs. For example, when documents concerning the politics are given, the system extracts "%" and "Cabinet approval rating" as a unit and an item expression including temporal expressions. It next extracts values related to "%". Finally, it makes a graph where temporal expressions are used for the horizontal axis and the value of percentage is shown on the vertical axis. This graph indicates the trend of Cabinet approval rating and is useful for investigating Cabinet approval rating. Graphs are obviously easy to recognize and useful for understanding information described in documents. In experiments, when we judged the extraction of a correct graph as the top output to be correct, the system accuracy was 0.2500 in evaluation A and 0.3334 in evaluation B. (In evaluation A, a graph where 75% or more of the points were correct was judged to be correct; in evaluation B, a graph where 50% or more of the points were correct was judged to be correct.) When we judged the extraction of a correct graph in the top five outputs to be correct, accuracy rose to 0.4167 in evaluation A and 0.6250 in evaluation B. Our system is convenient and effective because it can output a graph that includes trend information at these levels of accuracy when given only a set of documents as input.

1 Introduction

We have studied ways to automatically extract trend information from text documents, such as newspaper articles, because such a capability will be useful for exploring and examining trends. In this work, we used data sets provided by a workshop on multimodal summarization for trend information (the MuST Workshop) to construct an automatic trend exploration system. This system firsts extract units, temporals, and item expressions from newspaper articles, then it extract sets of expressions as trend information, and finally it arranges the sets and displays them in graphs. For example, when documents concerning the politics

Proceedings of the Workshop on Information Extraction Beyond The Document, pages 1–11,
Sydney, July 2006.

are given, the system extracts "%" and "Cabinet approval rating" as a unit and an item expression including temporal expressions. It next extracts values related to "%". Finally, it makes a graph where temporal expressions are used for the horizontal axis and the value of percentage is shown on the vertical axis. This graph indicates the trend of Cabinet approval rating and is useful for investigating Cabinet approval rating. Graphs are obviously easy to recognize and useful for understanding information described in documents.

2 The MuST Workshop

Kato et al. organized the workshop on multimodal summarization for trend information (the MuST Workshop) (Kato et al., 2005). In this workshop, participants were given data sets consisting of newspaper documents (editions of the Mainichi newspaper from 1998 and 1999 (Japanese documents)) that included trend information for various domains. In the data, tags for important expressions (e.g. temporals, numerical expressions, and item expressions) were tagged manually.[1] The 20 topics of the data sets (e.g., the 1998 home-run race to break the all-time Major League record, the approval rating for the Japanese Cabinet, and news on typhoons) were provided. Trend information was defined as information regarding the change in a value for a certain item. A change in the number of home runs hit by a certain player or a change in the approval rating for the Cabinet are examples of trend information. In the workshop, participants could freely use the data sets for any study they chose to do.

3 System

3.1 Structure of the system

Our automatic trend exploration system consists of the following components.

1. Component to extract important expressions

   First, documents related to a certain topic are given to the system, which then extracts important expressions that will be used to extract and merge trend information. The system extracts item units, temporal units, and item expressions as important expressions.

   Here, important expressions are defined as expressions that play important roles in a given document set. Item expressions are defined as expressions that are strongly related to the content of a given document set.

   1a. Component to extract important item units

   The system extracts item units that will be used to extract and merge trend information.

   For example, when documents concerning the home-run race are given, "*hon*" or "*gou*" (the Japanese item units for the number of home runs) such as in "54 *hon*" (54th home run) are extracted.

   1b. Component to extract important temporal units

   The system extracts temporal units that will also be used to extract and merge trend information.

   For example, the system extracts temporal units such as "*nichi*" (day), "*gatsu*" (month), and "*nen*" (year). In Japanese, temporal units are used to express dates, such as in "2006 *nen*, 3 *gatsu*, 27 *nichi*" for March 27th, 2006.

   1c. Component to extract important item expressions

   The system extracts item expressions that will also be used to extract and merge trend information.

   For example, the system extracts expressions that are objects for trend exploration, such as "McGwire" and "Sosa" as item expressions in the case of documents concerning the home-run race.

2. Component to extract trend information sets

   The system identifies the locations in sentences where a temporal unit, an item unit, and an item expression that was extracted by the component to extract important expressions appear in similar sentences and extracts sets of important expressions described by the sentences as a trend information set. The system also extracts numerical values appearing with item units or temporal units, and uses the connection of the numerical values and the item units or temporal units as numerical expressions or temporal expressions.

[1] We do not use manually provided tags for important expressions because our system automatically extracts important expressions.

For example, in the case of documents concerning the home-run race, the system extracts a set consisting of "item expression: McGwire", "temporal expression: 11 *day*" (the 11th), and "numerical expression: 47 *gou*" (47th home run) as a trend information set.

3. Component to extract and display important trend information sets

   The system gathers the extracted trend information sets and displays them as graphs or by highlighting text displays.

   For example, for documents concerning the home-run race, the system displays as graphs the extracted trend information sets for "McGwire" . In these graphs, temporal expressions are used for the horizontal axis and the number of home runs is shown on the vertical axis.

3.2 Component to extract important expressions

The system extracts important expressions that will be used to extract trend information sets. Important expressions belong to one of the following categories.

- item units
- temporal units
- item expressions

We use ChaSen (Matsumoto et al., 1999), a Japanese morphological analyzer, to extract expressions. Specifically, we use the parts of speeches in the ChaSen outputs to extract the expressions.

The system extracts item units, temporal units, and item expressions by using manually constructed rules using the parts of speeches. The system extracts a sequence of nouns adjacent to numerical values as item units. It then extracts expressions from among the item units which include an expression regarding time or date (e.g., "year", "month", "day", "hour", or "second") as temporal units. The system extracts a sequence of nouns as item expressions.

The system next extracts important item units, temporal units, and item expressions that play important roles in the target documents.

The following three methods can be used to extract important expressions. The system uses one of them. The system judges that an expression producing a high value from the following equations is an important expression.

- Equation for the TF numerical term in Okapi (Robertson et al., 1994)

$$Score = \sum_{i \in Docs} \frac{TF_i}{TF_i + \frac{l_i}{\Delta}} \quad (1)$$

- Use of total word frequency

$$Score = \sum_{i \in Docs} TF_i \quad (2)$$

- Use of total frequency of documents where a word appears

$$Score = \sum_{i \in Docs} 1 \quad (3)$$

In these equations, i is the ID (identification number) of a document, $Docs$ is a set of document IDs, TF_i is the occurrence number of an expression in document i, l is the length of document i, and Δ is the average length of documents in $Docs$.

To extract item expressions, we also applied a method that uses the product of the occurrence number of an expression in document i and the length of the expression as TF_i, so that we could extract longer expressions.

3.3 Component to extract trend information sets

The system identifies the locations in sentences where a temporal unit, an item unit, and an item expression extracted by the component to extract important expressions appears in similar sentences and extracts sets of important expressions described by the sentences as a trend information set. When more than one trend information set appears in a document, the system extracts the one that appears first. This is because important and new things are often described in the beginning of a document in the case of newspaper articles.

3.4 Component to extract and display important trend information sets

The system gathers the extracted trend information sets and displays them in graphs or as highlighted text. In the graphs, temporal expressions are used for the horizontal axis and numerical expressions are used for the vertical axis. The system also displays sentences used to extract trend information sets and highlights important expressions in the sentences.

The system extracts multiple item units, temporal units, and item expressions (through the component to extract important expressions) and uses these to make all possible combinations of the three kinds of expression. The system extracts trend information sets for each combination and calculates the value of one of the following equations for each combination. The system judges that the combination producing a higher value represents more useful trend information. The following four equations can be used for this purpose, and the system uses one of them.

- Method 1 — Use both the frequency of trend information sets and the scores of important expressions

$$M = Freq \times S_1 \times S_2 \times S_3 \quad (4)$$

- Method 2 — Use both the frequency of trend information sets and the scores of important expressions

$$M = Freq \times (S_1 \times S_2 \times S_3)^{\frac{1}{3}} \quad (5)$$

- Method 3 — Use the frequency of trend information sets

$$M = Freq \quad (6)$$

- Method 4 — Use the scores of important expressions

$$M = S_1 \times S_2 \times S_3 \quad (7)$$

In these equations, $Freq$ is the number of trend information sets extracted as described in Section 3.3, and $S1$, $S2$, and $S3$ are the values of $Score$ as calculated by the corresponding equation in Section 3.2.

The system extracts the top five item units, the top five item expressions, and the top three temporal units through the component to extract important expressions and forms all possible combinations of these (75 combinations). The system then calculates the value of the above equations for these 75 combinations and judges that a combination having a larger value represents more useful trend information.

4 Experiments and Discussion

We describe some examples of the output of our system in Sections 4.1, 4.2, and 4.3, and the results from our system evaluation in Section 4.4. We made experiments using Japanese newspaper articles.

4.1 Extracting important expressions

To extract important expressions we applied the equation for the TF numerical term in Okapi and the method using the product of the occurrence number for an expression and the length of the expression as TF_i for item expressions. We did experiments using the three document sets for typhoons, the Major Leagues, and political trends. The results are shown in Table 1.

We found that appropriate important expressions were extracted for each domain. For example, in the data set for typhoons, "typhoon" was extracted as an important item expression and an item unit "*gou*" (No.), indicating the ID number of each typhoon, was extracted as an important item unit. In the data set for the Major Leagues, the MuST data included documents describing the home-run race between Mark McGwire and Sammy Sosa in 1998. "McGwire" and "Sosa" were properly extracted among the higher ranks. "*gou*" (No.) and "*hon*" (home run(s)), important item units for the home-run race, were properly extracted. In the data set for political trends, "*naikaku shiji ritsu*" (cabinet approval rating) was properly extracted as an item expression and "%" was extracted as an item unit.

4.2 Graphs representing trend information

We next tested how well our system graphed the trend information obtained from the MuST data sets. We used the same three document sets as in the previous section. As important expressions in the experiments, we used the item unit, the temporal unit, and the item expression with the highest scores (the top ranked ones) which were extracted by the component to extract important expressions using the method described in the previous section. The system made the graphs using the component to extract trend information sets and the component to extract and display important trend information sets. The graphs thus produced are shown in Figs. 1, 2, and 3. (We used Excel to draw these graphs.) Here, we made a temporal axis for each temporal expression. However, we can also

Table 1: Examples of extracting important expressions

Typhoon		
item units	temporal units	item expressions
gou (No.)	*nichi* (day)	*taihuu* (typhoon)
me-toru (meter(s))	*ji* (o'clock)	*gogo* (afternoon)
nin (people)	*jigoro* (around x o'clock)	*higai* (damage)
kiro (kilometer(s))	*fun* (minute(s))	*shashin setsumei* (photo caption)
miri (millimeter(s))	*jisoku* (per hour)	*chuushin* (center)
Major League		
item units	temporal units	item expressions
gou (No.)	*nichi* (day)	*Maguwaia* (McGwire)
hon (home run(s))	*nen* (year)	*honruida* (home run)
kai (inning(s))	*gatsu* (month)	*Ka-jinarusu* (Cardinals)
honruida (home run(s))	*nen buri* (after x year(s) interval)	*Ma-ku Maguwaia ichiruishu* (Mark McGwire, the first baseman)
shiai (game(s))	*fun* (minute(s))	*So-sa* (Sosa)
Political Trend		
item units	temporal units	item expressions
% (%)	*gatsu* (month)	*naikaku shiji ritsu* (cabinet approval rating)
pointo gen (decrease of x point(s))	*nichi* (day)	*Obuchi naikaku* (Obuchi Cabinet)
pointo zou (increase of x point(s))	*nen* (year)	*Obuchi shushou* (Prime Minister Obuchi)
dai (generation)	*kagetu* (month(s))	*shijiritsu* (approval rating)
pointo (point(s))	*bun no* (divided)	*kitai* (expectation)

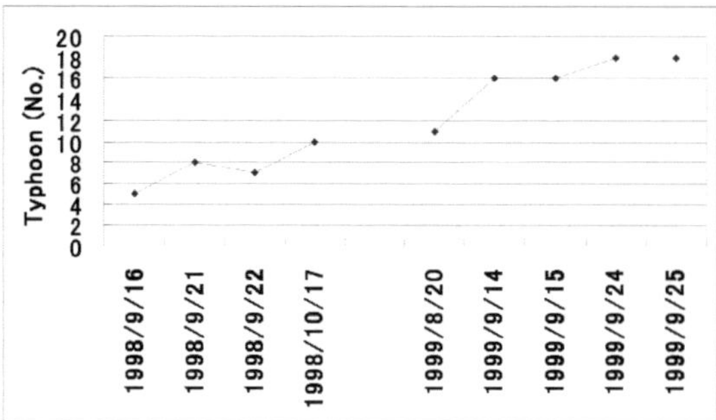

Figure 1: Trend graph for the typhoon data set

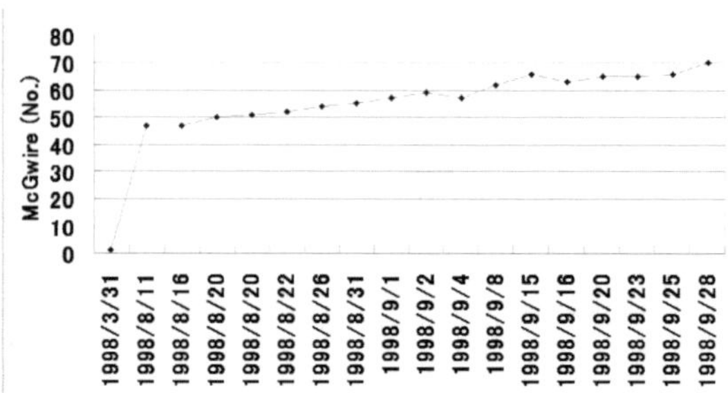

Figure 2: Trend graph for the Major Leagues data set

display a graph where regular temporal intervals are used in the temporal axis.

For the typhoon data set, *gou* (No.), *nichi* (day), and *taihuu* (typhoon) were respectively extracted as the top ranked item unit, temporal unit, and item expression. The system extracted trend information sets using these, and then made a graph where the temporal expression (day) was used for the horizontal axis and the ID numbers of the typhoons were shown on the vertical axis. The MuST data included data for September and October of 1998 and 1999. Figure 1 is useful for seeing when each typhoon hit Japan during the typhoon season each year. Comparing the 1998 data with that of 1999 reveals that the number of typhoons increased in 1999.

For the Major Leagues data set, *gou* (No.), *nichi* (day), and *Maguwaia* (McGwire) were extracted with the top rank. The system used these to make a graph where the temporal expression (day) was used for the horizontal axis and the cumulative number of home runs hit by McGwire was shown on the vertical axis (Fig. 2). The MuST data included data beginning in August, 1998. The graph shows some points where the cumulative number of home runs decreased (e.g., September

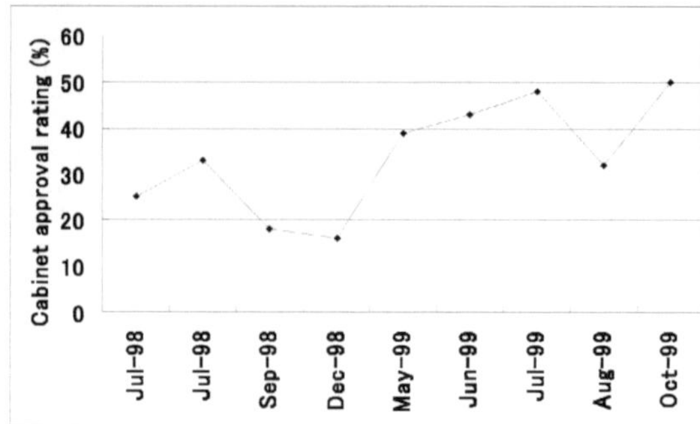

Figure 3: Trend graph for the political trends data set

4th), which was obviously incorrect. This was because our system wrongly extracted the number of home runs hit by Sosa when this was given close to McGwire's total.

In the political trends data set, %, *gatsu* (month), and *naikaku shiji ritsu* (cabinet approval rating) were extracted with the top rankings. The system used these to make a graph where the temporal expression (month) was used for the horizontal axis and the Cabinet approval rating (Japanese Cabinet) was shown as a percentage on the vertical axis. The MuST data covered 1998 and 1999. Figure 2 shows the cabinet approval rating of the Obuchi Cabinet. We found that the overall approval rating trend was upwards. Again, there were some errors in the extracted trend information sets. For example, although June was handled correctly, the system wrongly extracted May as a temporal expression from the sentence "in comparison to the previous investigation in May".

4.3 Sentence extraction and highlighting display

We then tested the sentence extraction and highlighting display with respect to trend information using the MuST data set; in this case, we used the typhoon data set. As important expressions, we used the item unit, the temporal unit, and the item expression extracted with the highest scores (the top ranked ones) by the component to extract important expressions using the method described in the previous section. *Gou* (No.), *nichi* (day), and *taihuu* (typhoon) were respectively extracted as an item unit, a temporal unit, and an item expression. The system extracted sentences including the three expressions and highlighted these expressions in the sentences. The results are shown in Figure 4. The first trend information sets to ap-

Sept. 16, 1998 No. 5 Large-scale and medium-strength Typhoon No. 5 made landfall near Omaezaki in Shizuoka Prefecture before dawn on the 16th, and then moved to the northeast involving the Koshin, Kantou, and Touhoku areas in the storm.
Sept. 21, 1998 No. 8 Small-scale Typhoon No. 8 made landfall near Tanabe City in Wakayama Prefecture around 4:00 p.m. on the 21st, and weakened while tracking to the northward across Kinki district.
Sept. 22, 1998 No. 7 Typhoon No. 7 made landfall near Wakayama City in the afternoon on the 22nd, and will hit the Kinki district.
Sept. 21, 1998 No. 8 The two-day consecutive landfall of Typhoon No. 8 on the 21st and Typhoon No. 7 on the 22nd caused nine deaths and many injuries in a total of six prefectures including Nara, Fukui, Shiga, and so on.
Oct. 17, 1998 No. 10 Medium-scale and medium-strength Typhoon No. 10 made landfall on Makurazaki City in Kagoshima Prefecture around 4:30 p.m. on the 17th, and then moved across the West Japan area after making another landfall near Sukumo City in Kochi Prefecture in the evening.
Aug. 20, 1999 No. 11 The Meteorological Office announced on the 20th that Typhoon No. 11 developed 120 kilometers off the south-southwest coast of Midway.
Sept. 14, 1999 No. 16 Typhoon No. 16, which developed off the south coast in Miyazaki Prefecture, made landfall near Kushima City in the prefecture around 5:00 p.m. on the 14th.
Sept. 15, 1999 No. 16 Small-scale and weak Typhoon No. 16 became extratropical in Nagano Prefecture and moved out to sea off Ibaraki Prefecture on the 15th.
Sept. 24, 1999 No. 18 Medium-scale and strong Typhoon No. 18 made landfall in the north of Kumamoto Prefecture around 6:00 a.m. on the 24th, and after moving to Suo-Nada made another landfall at Ube City in Yamaguchi Prefecture before 9:00 p.m., tracked through the Chugoku district, and then moved into the Japan Sea after 10:00 p.m.
Sept. 25, 1999 No. 18 Typhoon No. 18, which caused significant damage in the Kyushu and Chugoku districts, weakened and made another landfall before moving into the Sea of Okhotsk around 10:00 a.m. on the 25th.

Figure 4: Sentence extraction and highlighting display for the typhoon data set

pear are underlined twice and the other sets are underlined once. (In the actual system, color is used to make this distinction.) The extracted temporal expressions and numerical expressions are presented in the upper part of the extracted sentence. The graphs shown in the previous section were made by using these temporal expressions and numerical expressions.

The extracted sentences plainly described the state of affairs regarding the typhoons and were important sentences. For the research being done on summarization techniques, this can be considered a useful means of extracting important sentences. The extracted sentences typically describe the places affected by each typhoon and whether there was any damage. They contain important descriptions about each typhoon. This confirmed that a simple method of extracting sentences containing an item unit, a temporal unit, and an item expression can be used to extract important sentences.

The fourth sentence in the figure includes information on both typhoon no.7 and typhoon no.8. We can see that there is a trend information set other than the extracted trend information set (underlined twice) from the expressions that are underlined once. Since the system sometimes extracts incorrect trend information sets, the highlighting is useful for identifying such sets.

4.4 Evaluation

We used a closed data set and an open data set to evaluate our system. The closed data set was the data set provided by the MuST workshop organizer and contained 20 domain document sets. The data sets were separated for each domain.

We made the open data set based on the MuST data set using newspaper articles (editions of the Mainichi newspaper from 2000 and 2001). We made 24 document sets using information retrieval by term query. We used documents retrieved by term query as the document set of the domain for each query term.

We used the closed data set to adjust our system and used the open data set to calculate the evaluation scores of our system for evaluation.

We judged whether a document set included the information needed to make trend graphs by consulting the top 30 combinations of three kinds of important expression having the 30 highest values as in the method of Section 3.4. There were 19 documents including such information in the open data. We used these 19 documents for the following evaluation.

In the evaluation, we examined how accurately trend graphs could be output when using the top ranked expressions. The results are shown in Table 2. The best scores are described using bold fonts for each evaluation score.

We used five evaluation scores. MRR is the average of the score where $1/r$ is given as the score when the rank of the first correct output is r (Murata et al., 2005b). TP1 is the average of the precision in the first output. TP5 is the average of the precision where the system includes a correct output in the first five outputs. RP is the average of the r-precision and AP is the average of the average precision. (Here, the average means that the evaluation score is calculated for each domain data set and the summation of these scores divided by the number of the domain data sets is the average.) R-precision is the precision of the r outputs where r is the number of correct answers. Average precision is the average of the precision when each correct answer is output (Murata et al., 2000). The r-precision indicates the precision where the recall and the precision have the same value. The precision is the ratio of correct answers in the system output. The recall is the ratio of correct answers in the system output to the total number of correct answers.

Methods 1 to 4 in Table 2 are the methods used to extract useful trend information described in Section 3.4. Use of the expression length means the product of the occurrence number for an expression and the length of the expression was used to calculate the score for an important item expression. No use of the expression length means this product was not used and only the occurrence number was used.

To calculate the r-precision and average precision, we needed correct answer sets. We made the correct answer sets by manually examining the top 30 outputs for the 24 ($= 4 \times 6$) methods (the combinations of methods 1 to 4 and the use of Equations 1 to 3 with or without the expression length) and defining the useful trend information among them as the correct answer sets.

In evaluation A, a graph where 75% or more of the points were correct was judged to be correct. In evaluation B, a graph where 50% or more of the points were correct was judged to be correct.

Table 2: Experimental results for the open data

	Evaluation A					Evaluation B				
	MRR	TP1	TP5	RP	AP	MRR	TP1	TP5	RP	AP
Use of Equation 1 and the expression length										
Method 1	0.3855	**0.3158**	0.4737	0.1360	0.1162	0.5522	**0.4211**	0.7368	0.1968	0.1565
Method 2	0.3847	**0.3158**	0.4211	0.1360	0.1150	0.5343	**0.4211**	0.6316	0.1880	0.1559
Method 3	0.3557	0.2632	0.4211	0.1360	0.1131	0.5053	0.3684	0.6316	0.1805	0.1541
Method 4	0.3189	0.2632	0.4211	0.1125	0.0973	0.4492	0.3158	0.6316	0.1645	0.1247
Use of Equation 2 and the expression length										
Method 1	**0.3904**	**0.3158**	0.4737	**0.1422**	0.1154	**0.5746**	**0.4211**	0.7368	**0.2127**	0.1674
Method 2	0.3877	**0.3158**	0.4737	**0.1422**	0.1196	0.5544	**0.4211**	0.7368	**0.2127**	**0.1723**
Method 3	0.3895	**0.3158**	**0.5263**	**0.1422**	**0.1202**	0.5491	**0.4211**	**0.7895**	**0.2127**	0.1705
Method 4	0.2216	0.1053	0.3684	0.0846	0.0738	0.3765	0.2105	0.5789	0.1328	0.1043
Use of Equation 3 and the expression length										
Method 1	0.3855	**0.3158**	0.4737	0.1335	0.1155	0.5452	**0.4211**	0.7368	0.1943	0.1577
Method 2	0.3847	**0.3158**	0.4211	0.1335	0.1141	0.5256	**0.4211**	0.6316	0.1855	0.1555
Method 3	0.3570	0.2632	0.4737	0.1335	0.1124	0.4979	0.3684	0.6842	0.1780	0.1524
Method 4	0.3173	0.2632	0.4737	0.1256	0.0962	0.4652	0.3684	0.6316	0.1777	0.1293
Use of Equation 1 and no use of the expression length										
Method 1	0.3789	**0.3158**	0.4737	0.1294	0.1152	0.5456	**0.4211**	0.7368	0.2002	0.1627
Method 2	0.3750	**0.3158**	0.4211	0.1294	0.1137	0.5215	**0.4211**	0.6842	0.2002	0.1621
Method 3	0.3333	0.2632	0.4211	0.1119	0.1072	0.4798	0.3684	0.6842	0.1763	0.1552
Method 4	0.2588	0.1053	0.4737	0.1269	0.0872	0.3882	0.1579	0.6842	0.1833	0.1189
Use of Equation 2 and no use of the expression length										
Method 1	0.3277	0.2105	0.4737	0.1134	0.0952	0.4900	0.2632	**0.7895**	0.1779	0.1410
Method 2	0.3662	0.2632	0.4737	0.1187	0.1104	0.5417	0.3684	0.7368	0.1831	0.1594
Method 3	0.3504	0.2632	0.4737	0.1187	0.1116	0.5167	0.3684	0.7368	0.1884	0.1647
Method 4	0.1877	0.0526	0.3684	0.0775	0.0510	0.3131	0.1053	0.5263	0.1300	0.0879
Use of Equation 3 and no use of the expression length										
Method 1	0.3855	**0.3158**	0.4737	0.1335	0.1155	0.5452	**0.4211**	0.7368	0.1943	0.1577
Method 2	0.3847	**0.3158**	0.4211	0.1335	0.1141	0.5256	**0.4211**	0.6316	0.1855	0.1555
Method 3	0.3570	0.2632	0.4737	0.1335	0.1124	0.4979	0.3684	0.6842	0.1780	0.1524
Method 4	0.3173	0.2632	0.4737	0.1256	0.0962	0.4652	0.3684	0.6316	0.1777	0.1293

From the experimental results, we found that the method using the total frequency for a word (Equation 2) and the length of an expression was best for calculating the scores of important expressions.

Using the length of an expression was important. (The way of using the length of an expression was described in the last part of Section 3.2.) For example, when "Cabinet approval rating" appears in documents, a method without expression lengths extracts "rating". When the system extracts trend information sets using "rating", it extracts wrong information related to types of "rating" other than "Cabinet approval rating". This hinders the extraction of coherent trend information. Thus, it is beneficial to use the length of an expression when extracting important item expressions.

We also found that method 1 (using both the frequency of the trend information sets and the scores of important expressions) was generally the best.

When we judged the extraction of a correct graph as the top output in the experiments to be correct, our best system accuracy was 0.3158 in evaluation A and 0.4211 in evaluation B. When we judged the extraction of a correct graph in the top five outputs to be correct, the best accuracy rose to 0.5263 in evaluation A and 0.7895 in evaluation B. In terms of the evaluation scores for the 24 original data sets (these evaluation scores were multiplied by $19/24$), when we judged the extraction of a correct graph as the top output in the experiments to be correct, our best system accuracy was 0.3158 in evaluation A and 0.4211 in evaluation B. When we judged the extraction of a correct graph in the top five outputs to be correct, the best accuracy rose to 0.5263 in evaluation A and 0.7895 in evaluation B. Our system is convenient and effective because it can output a graph that includes trend information at these levels of accuracy when given only a set of documents as input.

As shown in Table 2, the best values for RP (which indicates the precision where the recall and the precision have the same value) and AP were 0.2127 and 0.1705, respectively, in evaluation B.

This RP value indicates that our system could extract about one out of five graphs among the correct answers when the recall and the precision had the same value.

5 Related studies

Fujihata et al. (Fujihata et al., 2001) developed a system to extract numerical expressions and their related item expressions by using syntactic information and patterns. However, they did not deal with the extraction of important expressions or gather trend information sets. In addition, they did not make a graph from the extracted expressions.

Nanba et al. (Nanba et al., 2005) took an approach of judging whether the sentence relationship indicates transition (trend information) or renovation (revision of information) and used the judgment results to extract trend information. They also constructed a system to extract numerical information from input numerical units and make a graph that includes trend information. However, they did not consider ways to extract item numerical units and item expressions automatically.

In contrast to these systems, our system automatically extracts item numerical units and item expressions that each play an important role in a given document set. When a document set for a certain domain is given, our system automatically extracts item numerical units and item expressions, then extracts numerical expressions related to these, and finally makes a graph based on the extracted numerical expressions. When a document set is given, the system automatically makes a graph that includes trend information. Our system also uses an original method of producing more than one graphs and selecting an appropriate graph among them using Methods 1 to 4, which Fujihata et al. and Namba et al. did not use.

6 Conclusion

We have studied the automatic extraction of trend information from text documents such as newspaper articles. Such extraction will be useful for exploring and examining trends. We used data sets provided by a workshop on multimodal summarization for trend information (the MuST Workshop) to construct our automatic trend exploration system. This system first extracts units, temporals, and item expressions from newspaper articles, then it extracts sets of expressions as trend information, and finally it arranges the sets and displays them in graphs.

In our experiments, when we judged the extraction of a correct graph as the top output to be correct, the system accuracy was 0.2500 in evaluation

A and 0.3334 in evaluation B. (In evaluation A, a graph where 75% or more of the points were correct was judged to be correct; in evaluation B, a graph where 50% or more of the points were correct was judged to be correct.) When we judged the extraction of a correct graph in the top five outputs to be correct, we obtained accuracy of 0.4167 in evaluation A and 0.6250 in evaluation B. Our system is convenient and effective because it can output a graph that includes trend information at these levels of accuracy when only a set of documents is provided as input.

In the future, we plan to continue this line of study and improve our system. We also hope to apply the method of using term frequency in documents to extract trend information as reported by Murata et al. (Murata et al., 2005a).

References

Katsuyuki Fujihata, Masahiro Shiga, and Tatsunori Mori. 2001. Extracting of numerical expressions by constraints and default rules of dependency structure. *Information Processing Society of Japan, WGNL 145*.

Tsuneaki Kato, Mitsunori Matsushita, and Noriko Kando. 2005. MuST: A workshop on multimodal summarization for trend information. *Proceedings of the Fifth NTCIR Workshop Meeting on Evaluation of Information Access Technologies: Information Retrieval, Question Answering and Cross-Lingual Information Access*.

Yuji Matsumoto, Akira Kitauchi, Tatsuo Yamashita, Yoshitaka Hirano, Hiroshi Matsuda, and Masayuki Asahara. 1999. Japanese morphological analysis system ChaSen version 2.0 manual 2nd edition.

Masaki Murata, Kiyotaka Uchimoto, Hiromi Ozaku, Qing Ma, Masao Utiyama, and Hitoshi Isahara. 2000. Japanese probabilistic information retrieval using location and category information. *The Fifth International Workshop on Information Retrieval with Asian Languages*, pages 81–88.

Masaki Murata, Koji Ichii, Qing Ma, Tamotsu Shirado, Toshiyuki Kanamaru, and Hitoshi Isahara. 2005a. Trend survey on Japanese natural language processing studies over the last decade. In *The Second International Joint Conference on Natural Language Processing, Companion Volume to the Proceedings of Conference including Posters/Demos and Tutorial Abstracts*.

Masaki Murata, Masao Utiyama, and Hitoshi Isahara. 2005b. Use of multiple documents as evidence with decreased adding in a Japanese question-answering system. *Journal of Natural Language Processing*, 12(2).

Hidetsugu Nanba, Yoshinobu Kunimasa, Shiho Fukushima, Teruaki Aizawa, and Manabu Okumura. 2005. Extraction and visualization of trend information based on the cross-document structure. *Information Processing Society of Japan, WGNL 168*, pages 67–74.

S. E. Robertson, S. Walker, S. Jones, M. M. Hancock-Beaulieu, and M. Gatford. 1994. Okapi at TREC-3. In *TREC-3*.

Comparing Information Extraction Pattern Models

Mark Stevenson and Mark A. Greenwood
Department of Computer Science
University of Sheffield
Sheffield, S1 4DP, UK
{marks,m.greenwood}@dcs.shef.ac.uk

Abstract

Several recently reported techniques for the automatic acquisition of Information Extraction (IE) systems have used dependency trees as the basis of their extraction pattern representation. These approaches have used a variety of pattern models (schemes for representing IE patterns based on particular parts of the dependency analysis). An appropriate model should be expressive enough to represent the information which is to be extracted from text without being overly complicated. Four previously reported pattern models are evaluated using existing IE evaluation corpora and three dependency parsers. It was found that one model, linked chains, could represent around 95% of the information of interest without generating an unwieldy number of possible patterns.

1 Introduction

A common approach to Information Extraction (IE) is to use patterns which match against text and identify items of interest. Patterns are applied to text which has undergone various levels of linguistic analysis, such as phrase chunking (Soderland, 1999) and full syntactic parsing (Gaizauskas et al., 1996). The approaches use different definitions of what constitutes a valid pattern. For example, the AutoSlog system (Riloff, 1993) uses patterns which match certain grammatical categories, mainly nouns and verbs, in phrase chunked text while Yangarber et al. (2000) use subject-verb-object tuples derived from a dependency parse. An appropriate pattern language must encode enough information about the text to be able to accurately identify the items of interest. However, it should not contain so much information as to be complex and impractical to apply.

Several recent approaches to IE have used patterns based on a dependency analysis of the input text (Yangarber, 2003; Sudo et al., 2001; Sudo et al., 2003; Bunescu and Mooney, 2005; Stevenson and Greenwood, 2005). These approaches have used a variety of pattern models (schemes for representing IE patterns based on particular parts of the dependency tree). For example, Yangarber (2003) uses just subject-verb-object tuples while Sudo et al. (2003) allow any subpart of the tree to act as an extraction pattern. The set of patterns allowed by the first model is a proper subset of the second and therefore captures less of the information contained in the dependency tree. Little analysis has been carried out into the appropriateness of each model. Sudo et al. (2003) compared three models in terms of their ability to identify event participants.

The choice of pattern model has an effect on the number of potential patterns. This has implications on the practical application for each approach, particularly when used for automatic acquisition of IE systems using learning methods (Yangarber et al., 2000; Sudo et al., 2003; Bunescu and Mooney, 2005). This paper evaluates the appropriateness of four pattern models in terms of the competing aims of expressive completeness (ability to represent information in text) and complexity (number of possible patterns). Each model is examined by comparing it against a corpus annotated with events and determining the proportion of those which it is capable of representing.

The remainder of this paper is organised as follows: a variety of dependency-tree-based IE pat-

Proceedings of the Workshop on Information Extraction Beyond The Document, pages 12–19,
Sydney, July 2006.

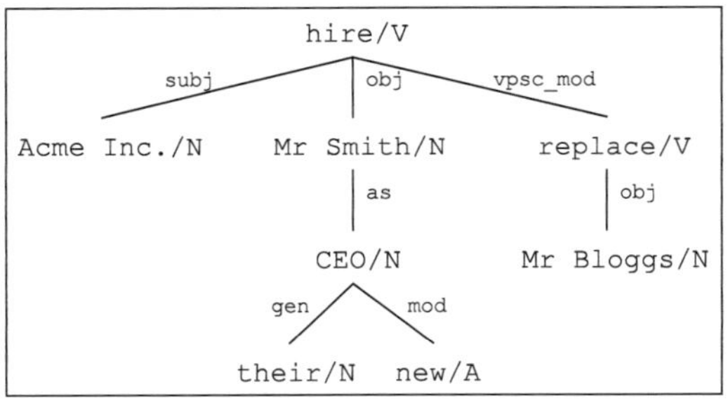

Figure 1: An example dependency tree.

tern models are introduced (Sections 2 and 3). Section 4 describes experiments comparing each model and the results are discussed in Section 5.

2 Pattern Models

In dependency analysis (Mel'čuk, 1987) the syntax of a sentence is represented by a set of directed binary links between a word (the head) and one of its modifiers. These links may be labelled to indicate the grammatical relation between the head and modifier (e.g. subject, object). In general cyclical paths are disallowed so that the analysis forms a tree structure. An example dependency analysis for the sentence *"Acme Inc. hired Mr Smith as their new CEO, replacing Mr Bloggs."* is shown Figure 1.

The remainder of this section outlines four models for representing extraction patterns which can be derived from dependency trees.

Predicate-Argument Model (SVO): A simple approach, used by Yangarber (2003) and Stevenson and Greenwood (2005), is to use subject-verb-object tuples from the dependency parse as extraction patterns. These consist of a verb and its subject and/or direct object[1]. An SVO pattern is extracted for each verb in a sentence. Figure 2 shows the two SVO patterns[2] which are produced for the dependency tree shown in Figure 1.

This model may be motivated by the assumption that many IE scenarios involve the extraction of participants in specific events. For example, the MUC-6 (MUC, 1995) management succession scenario concerns the identification of individuals who are changing job. These events are often described using a simple predicate argument structure, e.g. *"Acme Inc. fired Smith"*. However, the SVO model cannot represent information described using other linguistic constructions such as nominalisations or prepositional phrases. For example, in the MUC6 texts it is common for job titles to be mentioned within prepositional phrases, e.g. *"Smith joined Acme Inc. as CEO"*.

Chains: A pattern is defined as a path between a verb node and any other node in the dependency tree passing through zero or more intermediate nodes (Sudo et al., 2001). Figure 2 shows the eight chains which can be extracted from the tree in Figure 1.

Chains provide a mechanism for encoding information beyond the direct arguments of predicates and includes areas of the dependency tree ignored by the SVO model. For example, they can represent information expressed as a nominalisation or within a prepositional phrase, e.g. *"The resignation of Smith from the board of Acme ..."* However, a potential shortcoming of this model is that it cannot represent the link between arguments of a verb. Patterns in the chain model format are unable to represent even the simplest of sentences containing a transitive verb, e.g. *"Smith left Acme Inc."*.

Linked Chains: The linked chains model (Greenwood et al., 2005) represents extraction patterns as a pair of chains which share the same verb but no direct descendants. This model generates 14 patterns for the verb *hire* in Figure 1, examples of which are shown in Figure 2. This pattern representation encodes most of the information in the sentence with the advantage of being able to link together event participants which neither of the SVO or chain model can, for example the relation between *"Smith"* and *"Bloggs"*.

Subtrees: The final model to be considered is the subtree model (Sudo et al., 2003). In this model any subtree of a dependency tree can be used as an extraction pattern, where a subtree is any set of nodes in the tree which are connected to one another. Single nodes are not considered to be subtrees. The subtree model is a richer representation than those discussed so far and can represent any part of a dependency tree. Each of the previ-

[1]Yangarber et al. (2000) and Sudo et al. (2003) used a slightly extended version of this model in which the pattern also included certain phrases which referred to either the subject or object.

[2]The formalism used for representing dependency patterns is similar to the one introduced by Sudo et al. (2003). Each node in the tree is represented in the format `a[b/c]` (e.g. `subj[N/bomber]`) where `c` is the lexical item (`bomber`), `b` its grammatical tag (`N`) and `a` the dependency relation between this node and its parent (`subj`). The relationship between nodes is represented as `X(A+B+C)` which indicates that nodes `A`, `B` and `C` are direct descendents of node `X`.

SVO

```
[V/hire](subj[N/Acme Inc.]+obj[N/Mr Smith])
[V/replace](obj[N/Mr Bloggs])
```

Chains

```
[V/hire](subj[N/Acme Inc.])
[V/hire](obj[N/Mr Smith])
[V/hire](obj[N/Mr Smith](as[N/CEO]))
[V/hire](obj[N/Mr Smith](as[N/CEO](gen[N/their])))
[V/hire](obj[N/Mr Smith](as[N/CEO](mod[A/new])))
[V/hire](vpsc_mod[V/replace])
[V/hire](vpsc_mod[V/replace](obj[N/Mr Bloggs]))
[V/replace](obj[N/Mr Bloggs])
```

Linked Chains

```
[V/hire](subj[N/Acme Inc.]+obj[N/Mr Smith])
[V/hire](subj[N/Acme Inc.]+obj[N/Mr Smith](as[N/CEO]))
[V/hire](obj[N/Mr Smith]+vpsc_mod[V/replace](obj[N/Mr Bloggs]))
```

Figure 2: Example patterns for three models

ous models form a proper subset of the subtrees. By choosing an appropriate subtree it is possible to link together any pair of nodes in a tree and consequently this model can represent the relation between any set of items in the sentence.

3 Pattern Enumeration and Complexity

In addition to encoding different parts of the dependency analysis, each pattern model will also generate a different number of potential patterns.

A dependency tree, T, can be viewed as a set of N connected nodes. Assume that V, such that $V \subseteq N$, is the set of nodes in the dependency tree labelled as a verb.

Predicate-Argument Model (SVO): The number of SVO patterns extracted from T is:

$$N_{svo}(T) = |V| \quad (1)$$

Chain Model: A chain can be created between any verb and a node it dominates (directly or indirectly). Now assume that $d(v)$ denotes the count of a node v and all its descendents then the number of chains is given by:

$$N_{chains}(T) = \sum_{v \in V} (d(v) - 1) \quad (2)$$

Linked Chains: Let $C(v)$ denote the set of direct child nodes of node v and v_i denote the i-th child, so $C(v) = \{v_1, v_2, ...v_{|C(v)|}\}$. The number of possible linked chains in T is given by:

$$N_{linked chains}(T) = \sum_{v \in V} \sum_{i=1}^{|C(v)|} \sum_{j=i+1}^{|C(v)|} d(v_i)\, d(v_j) \quad (3)$$

Subtrees: Now assume that $sub(n)$ is a function denoting the number of subtrees, including single nodes, rooted at node n. This can be defined recursively as follows:

$$sub(n) = \begin{cases} 1 & \text{if } n \text{ is a leaf node} \\ \prod_{i=1}^{|C(n)|} (sub(n_i) + 1) & \text{otherwise} \end{cases} \quad (4)$$

The total number of subtrees in a tree is given by:

$$N_{subtree}(T) = \left(\sum_{n \in N} sub(n) \right) - |N| \quad (5)$$

The dependency tree shown in Figure 1 generates 2, 8, 14 and 42 possible SVO, chain, linked chain and subtree patterns respectively. The number of SVO patterns is constant on the number of verbs in the tree. The number of chains is generally a linear function on the size of the tree but, in the worst case, can be polynomial. The linked chain model generates a polynomial number of patterns while the subtree model is exponential.

There is a clear tradeoff between the complexity of pattern representations and the practicality of computation using them. Some pattern representations are more expressive, in terms of the amount of information from the dependency tree they make use of, than others (Section 2) and are therefore more likely to produce accurate extraction patterns. However, the more expressive models will add extra complexities during computation since a greater number of patterns will be generated. This complexity, both in the number of patterns produced and the computational effort required to produce them, limits the algorithms that can reasonably be applied to learn useful extraction patterns.

For a pattern model to be suitable for an extraction task it needs to be expressive enough to encode enough information from the dependency parse to accurately identify the items which need to be extracted. However, we also aim for the model to be as computationally tractable as possible. The ideal model will then be one with sufficient expressive power while at the same time not including extra information which would make its use less practical.

4 Experiments

We carried out experiments to determine how suitable the pattern representations detailed in Section 2 are for encoding the information of interest to IE systems. We chose a set of IE corpora annotated with the information to be extracted (detailed in Section 4.1), generated sets of patterns using a variety of dependency parsers (Section 4.2) which were then examined to discover how much of the target information they contain (Section 4.3).

4.1 Corpora

Corpora representing different genres of text were chosen for these experiments; one containing newspaper text and another composed of biomedical abstracts. The first corpus consisted of Wall Street Journal texts from the Sixth Message Understanding Conference (MUC, 1995) IE evaluation. These are reliably annotated with details about the movement of executives between jobs. We make use of a version of the corpus produced by Soderland (1999) in which events described within a single sentence were annotated. Events in this corpus identify relations between up to four entities: `PersonIn` (the person starting a new job), `PersonOut` (person leaving a job), `Post` (the job title) and `Organisation` (the employer). These events were broken down into a set of binary relationships. For example, the sentence *"Smith was recently made chairman of Acme."* contains information about the new employee (*Smith*), post (*chairman*) and organisation (*Acme*). Events are represented as a set of binary relationships, `Smith-chairman`, `chairman-Acme` and `Smith-Acme` for this example.

The second corpus uses documents taken from the biomedical domain, specifically the training corpus used in the LLL-05 challenge task (Nédellec, 2005), and a pair of corpora (Craven and Kumlien, 1999) which were derived from the Yeast Proteome Database (YPD) (Hodges et al., 1999) and the Online Mendelian Inheritance in Man database (OMIM) (Hamosh et al., 2002). Each of these corpora are annotated with binary relations between pairs of entities. The LLL-05 corpora contains interactions between genes and proteins. For example the sentence *"Expression of the sigma(K)-dependent cwlH gene depended on gerE"* contains relations between *sigma(K)* and *cwlH* and between *gerE* and *cwlH*. The YPD corpus is concerned with the subcellular compartments in which particular yeast proteins localize. An example sentence *"Uba2p is located largely in the nucleus"* relates *Uba2p* and *the nucleus*. The relations in the OMIM corpora are between genes and diseases, for example *"Most sporadic colorectal cancers also have two APC mutations"* contains a relation between *APC* and *colorectal cancer*.

The MUC6 corpus contains a total of six possible binary relations. Each of the three biomedical corpora contain a single relation type, giving a total of nine binary relations for the experiments. There are 3911 instances of binary relations in all corpora.

4.2 Generating Dependency Patterns

Three dependency parsers were used for these experiments: MINIPAR[3] (Lin, 1999), the Machinese Syntax[4] parser from Connexor Oy (Tapanainen and Järvinen, 1997) and the Stanford[5] parser (Klein and Manning, 2003). These three parsers represent a cross-section of approaches to producing dependency analyses: MINIPAR uses a constituency grammar internally before converting the result to a dependency tree, Machinese Syntax uses a functional dependency grammar, and the Stanford Parser is a lexicalized probabilistic parser.

Before these parsers were applied to the various corpora the named entities participating in relations are replaced by a token indicating their class. For example, in the MUC6 corpus *"Acme hired Smith"* would become "`Organisation` *hired* `PersonIn`". Each parser was adapted to deal with these tokens correctly. The parsers were applied to each corpus and patterns extracted from the dependency trees generated.

The analyses produced by the parsers were post-processed to make the most of the information they contain and ensure consistent structures from which patterns could be extracted. It was found

[3] `http://www.cs.ualberta.ca/~lindek/`

[4] `http://www.connexor.com/software/syntax/`

[5] `http://www-nlp.stanford.edu/software/`

Parser	SVO	Chains	Linked chains	Subtrees
MINIPAR	2,980	52,659	149,504	353,778,240,702,149,000
Machinese Syntax	2,382	67,690	265,631	4,641,825,924
Stanford	2,950	76,620	478,643	1,696,259,251,073

Table 1: Number of patterns produced for each pattern model by different parsers

that the parsers were often unable to generate a dependency tree which included the whole sentence and instead generate an analysis consisting of sentence fragments represented as separate tree structures. Some fragments did not include a verb so no patterns could be extracted. To take account of this we allowed the root node of any tree fragment to take the place of a verb in a pattern (see Section 2). This leads to the generation of more chain and linked chain patterns but has no effect on the number of SVO patterns or subtrees.

Table 1 shows the number of patterns generated from the dependency trees produced by each of the parsers. The number of subtrees generated from the MINIPAR parses is several orders of magnitude higher than the others because MINIPAR allows certain nodes to be the modifier of two separate nodes to deal with phenomena such as conjunction, anaphora and VP-coordination. For example, in the sentence *"The bomb caused widespread damage and killed three people" the bomb* is the subject of both the verbs *cause* and *kill*. We made use of this information by duplicating any nodes (and their descendants) with more than one head.[6]

Overall the figures in Table 1 are consistent with the analysis in Section 3 but there is great variation in the number of patterns produced by the different parsers. For example, the Stanford parser produces more chains and linked chains than the other parsers. (If we did not duplicate portions of the MINIPAR parses then the Stanford parser would also generate the most subtrees.) We found that the Stanford parser was the most likely to generate a single dependency tree for each sentence while the other two produced a set of tree fragments. A single dependency analysis contains a greater number of patterns, and possible subtrees, than a fragmented analysis. One reason for this may be that the Stanford parser is unique in allowing the use of an underspecified dependency relation, `dep`, which can be applied when the role of the dependency is unclear. This allows the Stanford parser to generate analyses which span more of the sentence than the other two.

4.3 Evaluating Pattern Models

Patterns from each of the four models are examined to check whether they cover the information which should be extracted. In this context "cover" means that the pattern contains both elements of the relation. For example, an SVO pattern extracted from the dependency parse of *"Smith was recently made chairman of Acme."* would be `[V/make](subj[N/Smith]+obj[N/chairman])` which covers the relation between *Smith* and *chairman* but not the relations between *Smith* and *Acme* or *chairman* and *Acme*. The coverage of each model is computed as the percentage of relations in the corpus for which at least one of the patterns contains both of the participating entities. Coverage is related to the more familiar IE evaluation metric of recall since the coverage of a pattern model places an upper bound on the recall of any system using that model. The aim of this work is to determine the proportion of the relations in a corpus that can be represented using the various pattern models rather than their performance in an IE system and, consequently, we choose to evaluate models in terms of their coverage rather than precision and recall.[7]

For practical applications parsers are required to generate the dependency analysis but these may not always provide a complete analysis for every sentence. The coverage of each model is influenced by the ability of the parser to produce a tree which connects the elements of the event to be extracted. To account for this we compute the coverage of each model relative to a particular parser. The subtree model covers all events whose entities are included in the dependency tree and, consequently, the coverage of this model represents the maximum number of events that the model can

[6] One dependency tree produced by MINIPAR, expanded in this way, contained approximately 1×10^{64} subtrees. These are not included in the total number of subtrees for the MINIPAR parses shown in the table.

[7] The subtree model can be used to cover any set of items in a dependency tree. So, given accurate dependency analyses, this model will cover all events. The coverage of the subtree model can be determined by checking if the elements of the event are connected in the dependency analysis of the sentence and, for simplicity, we chose to do this rather than enumerating all subtrees.

represent for a given dependency tree. The coverage of other models relative to a dependency analysis can be computed by dividing the number of events it covers by the number covered by the subtree model (i.e. the maximum which can be covered). This measure is refered to as the bounded coverage of the model. Bounded coverage for the subtree model is always 100%.

5 Results

Coverage and bounded-coverage results for each pattern representation and parser combination are given in Table 2. The table lists the corpus, the total number of instances within that corpus and the results for each of the four pattern models. Results for the subtree model lists the coverage and raw count, the bounded-coverage for this model will always be 100% and is not listed. Results for the other three models show the coverage and raw count along with the bounded coverage. The coverage of each parser and pattern representation (combined across both corpora) are also summarised in Figure 3.

The simplest representation, SVO, does not perform well in this evaluation. The highest bounded-coverage score is 15.1% (MUC6 corpus, Stanford parser) but the combined average over all corpora is less than 6% for any parser. This suggests that the SVO representation is simply not expressive enough for IE. Previous work which has used this representation have used indirect evaluation: document and sentence filtering (Yangarber, 2003; Stevenson and Greenwood, 2005). While the SVO representation may be expressive enough to allow a classifier to distinguish documents or sentences which are relevant to a particular extraction task it seems too limited to be used for relation extraction. The SVO representation performs noticeably worse on the biomedical text. Our analysis suggests that this is because the items of interest are commonly described in ways which the SVO model is unable to represent.

The more complex chain model covers a greater percentage of the relations. However its bounded-coverage is still less than half of the relations in either the MUC6 corpus or the biomedical texts. Using the chain model the best coverage which can be achieved over any corpus is 41.07% (MUC6 corpus, MINIPAR and Stanford parser) which is unlikely to be sufficient to create an IE system.

Results for the linked chain representation are much more promising covering around 70% of all relations using the MINIPAR and Machinese Syntax parsers and over 90.64% using the Stanford parser. For all three parsers this model achieves a bounded-coverage of close to 95%, indicating that this model can represent the majority of relations which are included in a dependency tree. The subtree representation covers slight more of the relations than linked chains: around 75% using the MINIPAR or Machinese Syntax parsers and 96.62% using the Stanford parser.

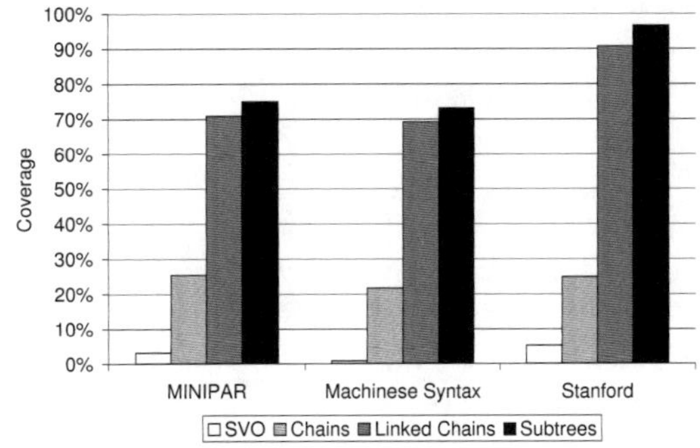

Figure 3: Coverage of various pattern representation models for each of the three parsers.

A one-way repeated measures ANOVA was carried out to analyse the differences between the results for each model shown in Table 2. It was found that the differences between the SVO, chain, linked chain and subtree models are significant ($p < 0.01$). A Tukey test was then applied to identify which of the individual differences between pairs of models were significant. Differences between two pairs of models were not found to be significant ($p < 0.01$): SVO and chains; linked chains and subtrees.

These results suggest that the linked chains and subtree models can represent significantly more of the relations which occur in IE scenarios than either the SVO or chain models. However, there is little to be gained from using the subtree model since accuracy of the linked chain model is comparable and the number of patterns generated is bounded by a polynomial rather than exponential function.

5.1 Analysis and Discussion

Examination of the relations which were covered by the subtree model but not by linked chains suggested that there are certain constructions which cause difficulties. One such construction is the appositive, e.g. the relation between

Parser	Corpus	# of Relations	SVO %C	SVO %B-C	Chains %C	Chains %B-C	Linked Chains %C	Linked Chains %B-C	Subtrees %C
MINIPAR	MUC6	1322	7.49 (99)	9.07	41.07 (543)	49.73	81.92 (1083)	99.18	82.60 (1092)
	Biomed	2589	0.93 (24)	1.30	17.38 (450)	24.44	65.31 (1691)	91.85	71.11 (1841)
	Combined	3911	3.14 (123)	4.19	25.39 (993)	33.86	70.93 (2774)	94.58	74.99 (2933)
Machinese Syntax	MUC6	1322	2.12 (28)	2.75	35.70 (472)	46.41	76.32 (1009)	99.21	76.93 (1017)
	Biomed	2589	0.19 (5)	0.27	14.56 (377)	20.47	65.47 (1695)	92.02	71.15 (1842)
	Combined	3911	0.84 (33)	1.15	21.71 (849)	29.70	69.14 (2704)	94.58	73.10 (2859)
Stanford	MUC6	1322	15.05 (199)	15.10	41.07 (543)	41.20	94.78 (1253)	95.07	99.70 (1318)
	Biomed	2589	0.46 (12)	0.49	16.53 (428)	17.39	88.52 (2292)	93.13	95.06 (2461)
	Combined	3911	5.40 (211)	5.58	24.83 (971)	25.69	90.64 (3545)	93.81	96.62 (3779)

Table 2: Evaluation results for the three different parsers.

`PersonOut` and `Organisation` in the fragment "`Organisation`*'s* `Post, PersonOut,` *resigned yesterday morning*". Certain nominalisations may also cause problems for the linked chains representation, e.g. in biomedical text the relation between `Agent` and `Target` in the nominalisation *"the* `Agent`*-dependent assembly of* `Target`*"* cannot be represented by a linked chain. In both cases the problem is caused by the fact that the dependency tree generated includes the two named entities in part of the tree dominated by a node marked as a noun. Since each linked chain must be anchored at a verb (or the root of a tree fragment) and the two chains cannot share part of their path, these relations are not covered. It would be possible to create another representation which allowed these relations to be captured but it would generate more patterns than the linked chain model.

Our results also reveal that the choice of dependency parser effects the coverage of each model (see Figure 3). The subtree model coverage scores for each parser shown in Table 3 represent the percentage of sentences for which an analysis was generated that included both items from the binary relations. These figures are noticably higher for the Stanford parser. We previously mentioned (Section 4.2) that this parser allows the use of an underspecified dependency relation and suggested that this may be a reason for the higher coverage. The use of underspecified dependency relations may not be useful for all applications but is unlikely to cause problems for systems which learn IE patterns provided the trees generated by the parser are consistent. Differences between the results produced by the three parsers suggest that it is important to fully evaluate their suitability for a particular purpose.

These experiments also provide insights into the more general question of how suitable dependency trees are as a basis for extraction patterns. Dependency analysis has the advantage of generating analyses which abstract away from the surface realisation of text to a greater extent than phrase structure grammars tend to. This leads to the semantic information being more accessible in the representation of the text which can be useful for IE. For practical applications this approach relies on the ability to accurately generate dependency analyses. The results presented here suggest that the Stanford parser (Klein and Manning, 2003) is capable of generating analyses for almost all sentences within corpora from two very different domains. Bunescu and Mooney (2005) have also demonstrated that dependency graphs can be produced using Combinatory Categorial Grammar (CCG) and context-free grammar (CFG) parsers.

6 Conclusions

This paper compares four IE pattern models: SVO, chains, linked chains and subtrees. Using texts from the management succession and biomedical domains it was found that the linked chains model can represent around 95% of the possible relations contained in the text, given a dependency parse. Subtrees can represent all the relations contained within dependency trees but their use is less practical because enumerating all possible subtrees is a more complex problem and the large number of resulting patterns could limit the learning algorithms that can be applied. This result should be borne in mind during the design of IE systems.

Acknowledgements

The authors are grateful to Mike Stannet for providing the method for counting subtrees introduced in Section 3 and to Connexor Oy for use of the Machinese Syntax parser. The research described in this paper was funded by the Engineering and Physical Sciences Research Council via the RESuLT project (GR/T06391) and partially funded by the IST 6th Framework project X-Media (FP6-26978).

References

Razvan Bunescu and Raymond Mooney. 2005. A shortest path dependency kernel for relation extraction. In *Proceedings of the Human Language Technology Conference and Conference on Empirical Methods in Natural Language Processing*, pages 724–731, Vancouver, B.C.

Mark Craven and Johan Kumlien. 1999. Constructing Biological Knowledge Bases by Extracting Information from Text Sources. In *Proceedings of the Seventh International Conference on Intelligent Systems for Molecular Biology*, pages 77–86, Heidelberg, Germany. AAAI Press.

Robert Gaizauskas, Takahiro Wakao, Kevin Humphreys, Hamish Cunningham, and Yorick Wilks. 1996. Description of the LaSIE system as used for MUC-6. In *Proceedings of the Sixth Message Understanding Conference (MUC-6)*, pages 207–220, San Francisco, CA.

Mark A. Greenwood, Mark Stevenson, Yikun Guo, Henk Harkema, and Angus Roberts. 2005. Automatically Acquiring a Linguistically Motivated Genic Interaction Extraction System. In *Proceedings of the 4th Learning Language in Logic Workshop (LLL05)*, Bonn, Germany.

Ada Hamosh, Alan F. Scott, Joanna Amberger, Carol Bocchini, David Valle, and Victor A. McKusick. 2002. Online Mendelian Inheritance in Man (OMIM), a knowledgebase of human genes and genetic disorders. *Nucleic Acids Research*, 30(1):52–55.

Peter E. Hodges, Andrew H. Z. McKee, Brian P. Davis, William E. Payne, and James I. Garrels. 1999. The Yeast Proteome Database (YPD): a model for the organization and presentation of genome-wide functional data. *Nucleic Acids Research*, 27(1):69–73.

Dan Klein and Christopher D. Manning. 2003. Accurate Unlexicalized Parsing. In *Proceedings of the 41st Annual Meeting of the Association for Computational Linguistics (ACL-03)*, pages 423–430, Sapporo, Japan.

Dekang Lin. 1999. MINIPAR: A Minimalist Parser. In *Maryland Linguistics Colloquium*, University of Maryland, College Park.

Igor Mel'čuk. 1987. *Dependency Syntax: Theory and Practice*. SUNY Press, New York.

MUC. 1995. *Proceedings of the Sixth Message Understanding Conference (MUC-6)*, San Mateo, CA. Morgan Kaufmann.

Claire Nédellec. 2005. Learning Language in Logic - Genic Interaction Extraction Challenge. In *Proceedings of the 4th Learning Language in Logic Workshop (LLL05)*, Bonn, Germany, August.

Ellen Riloff. 1993. Automatically constructing a dictionary for information extraction tasks. pages 811–816.

Stephen Soderland. 1999. Learning Information Extraction Rules for Semi-structured and free text. *Machine Learning*, 31(1-3):233–272.

Mark Stevenson and Mark A. Greenwood. 2005. A Semantic Approach to IE Pattern Induction. In *Proceedings of the 43rd Annual Meeting of the Association for Computational Linguistics*, pages 379–386, Ann Arbor, MI.

Kiyoshi Sudo, Satoshi Sekine, and Ralph Grishman. 2001. Automatic Pattern Acquisition for Japanese Information Extraction. In *Proceedings of the Human Language Technology Conference (HLT2001)*.

Kiyoshi Sudo, Satoshi Sekine, and Ralph Grishman. 2003. An Improved Extraction Pattern Representation Model for Automatic IE Pattern Acquisition. In *Proceedings of the 41st Annual Meeting of the Association for Computational Linguistics (ACL-03)*, pages 224–231, Sapporo, Japan.

Pasi Tapanainen and Timo Järvinen. 1997. A Non-Projective Dependency Parser. In *Proceedings of the 5th Conference on Applied Natural Language Processing*, pages 64–74, Washington, DC.

Roman Yangarber, Ralph Grishman, Pasi Tapanainen, and Silja Huttunen. 2000. Automatic Acquisition of Domain Knowledge for Information Extraction. In *Proceedings of the 18th International Conference on Computational Linguistics (COLING 2000)*, pages 940–946, Saarbrücken, Germany.

Roman Yangarber. 2003. Counter-training in the Discovery of Semantic Patterns. In *Proceedings of the 41st Annual Meeting of the Association for Computational Linguistics (ACL-03)*, pages 343–350, Sapporo, Japan.

Automatic Extraction of Definitions from German Court Decisions

Stephan Walter
Department of Computational Linguistics
Universität des Saarlandes
66123 Saarbrücken, Germany
stwa@coli.uni-saarland.de

Manfred Pinkal
Department of Computational Linguistics
Universität des Saarlandes
66123 Saarbrücken, Germany
pinkal@coli.uni-saarland.de

Abstract

This paper deals with the use of computational linguistic analysis techniques for information access and ontology learning within the legal domain. We present a rule-based approach for extracting and analysing definitions from parsed text and evaluate it on a corpus of about 6000 German court decisions. The results are applied to improve the quality of a text based ontology learning method on this corpus.[1]

1 Motivation

Methods like ontology based knowledge management and information access through conceptual search have become active research topics in the general research community, with practical applications in many areas. However the use of IT in legal practice (at least in German speaking countries) is up to now mainly restricted to document preparation and management or Boolean keyword search on full-text collections. Legal ontologies have been proposed in various research projects, but they focus on an upper level of concepts and are, with only a few exceptions, small knowledge repositories that were hand-made by experts (for a summary of existing legal ontologies, cf. (Valente 2004)).

It is clear that realistically large knowledge-based applications in the legal domain will need more comprehensive ontologies incorporating e.g. up-to-date knowledge from court decisions. For this purpose an expert-based approach has to be supplemented by automatic acquisition methods. The same is true for large-scale advanced information access: Extensive conceptual indexation of even a fraction of all court decisions published in one year seems hardly possible without automatic support. However there has been relatively little research on the use of natural language processing for this purpose (exceptions are (Lame 2005) and (Saias and Quaresma 2005)).

In this paper we look at the use of computational linguistic analysis techniques for information access and ontology learning within the legal domain. We present a rule-based method for extracting and analyzing definitions from parsed text, and evaluate this method on a corpus of about 6000 German court decisions within the field of environmental law. We then report on an experiment exploring the use of our extraction results to improve the quality of text-based ontology learning from noun-adjective bigrams. We will start however with a general discussion of the role that definitions play in legal language.

2 Definitions in Legal Language

Two central kinds of knowledge contained in the statutes of a code law system are *normative knowledge*, connecting legal consequences to descriptions of certain facts and situations, and *terminological knowledge*, consisting in definitions of some of the concepts used in these descriptions (Valente and Breuker 1994).

Normative content is exemplified by (1), parts of section 324a of the German criminal law. The legal consequence consisting in the specified punishment is connected to the precondition of soil pollution:

(1) Whoever (...) allows to penetrate or releases substances into the soil and thereby pollutes it or otherwise detrimentally alters it:

[1] This paper describes research within the project CORTE funded by the German Science Foundation, DFG PI 154/10-1 (http://www.coli.uni-saarland.de/projects/corte/)

Proceedings of the Workshop on Information Extraction Beyond The Document, pages 20–28,
Sydney, July 2006. ©2006 Association for Computational Linguistics

1. in a manner that is capable of harming (...) property of significant value or a body of water (...)

shall be punished with imprisonment for not more than five years or a fine.

Terminological knowledge consists in definitions of concepts used to describe the sanctioned facts. E.g., *soil* is defined in article 2 of the German soil protection law as follows:

(2) *Soil within the meaning of this Act is the upper layer of the earth's crust (...) including its liquid components (soil solution) and gaseous components (soil air), except groundwater and beds of bodies of water.*

If the definitions contained in statutes would fully specify how the relevant concepts are to be applied, cases could be solved (once the relevant statutes have been identified) by mechanically checking which of some given concepts apply, and then deriving the appropriate legal consequences in a logical conclusion. However such a simple procedure is never possible in reality. Discussions in courts (and consequently in all legal texts that document court decisions) are in large parts devoted to pinning down whether certain concepts apply. Controversies often arise because not all relevant concepts are defined at all within statutes, and because the terms used in legal definitions are often in need of clarification themselves. For instance it may be unclear in some cases what exactly counts as the *bed of a body of water* mentioned in Example (2). Additionally, reality is complex and constantly changing, and these changes also pertain to the applicability of formerly clear-cut concepts. While this is especially true of social reality, rather physical concepts may also be affected. An often cited example is a case where the German *Reichsgericht* had to decide whether *electricity* was to be counted as a *thing*.

At the heart of these difficulties lies the fact that statutes are written in natural language, not in a formalized or a strongly restricted specialized language. It is widely assumed in the philosophical literature that most natural language concepts do not lend themselves to definitions fixing all potential conditions of applicability a priori. From the point of view of legal theory this open-textured character of natural language concepts is often seen as essential for the functioning of any legal system (the term open texture was introduced into this discussion by (Hart 1961)). The use of natural language expressions allows for a continuous re-adjustment of the balance between precision and openness. This possibility is needed to provide regulations that are on the one hand reliable and on the other hand flexible enough to serve as a common ground for all kinds of social interaction. For the solution of concrete cases, the concepts made available within statute texts are supplemented by further definitions (in a wide sense, covering all kinds of modification and adaptation of concepts) given in the courts' decisions (in particular within the reasons for judgement). Such definitions for instance fix whether a certain stretch of sand counts as the *bed of a body of water* or if something is of *significant value* in the case at hand. These definitions are generally open for later amendment or revision. Still they almost always remain binding beyond the case at hand.

Easy access to definitions in decisions is therefore of great importance to the legal practitioner. Sections 3 and 4 show how computational linguistic analysis helps answering this need by enabling an accurate search for definitions in a large collection of court decisions. Accurate definition extraction is a prerequisite to building up an information system that allows for concept-centred access to the interpretational knowledge spread over tens of thousands of documents produced by courts every year.

Definitions are however not only of direct value as a source of information in legal practice. They also provide contexts that contain particularly much relevant terminology, and are therefore a good place to search for concepts to be integrated in a domain ontology. Given the importance and frequency of definitions in legal text, such an approach seems particularly promising for this domain. Section 5 describes how automatically extracted definitions improve the results of a standard ontology learning method.

3 Structure of Definitions

Our current work is based on a collection of more than 6000 verdicts in environmental law. As a starting point however we conducted a survey based on a random selection of 40 verdicts from various legal fields (none of them is in our present test set), which contained 130 definitions. Inspection of these definitions has shown a range of common structural elements, and has allowed us to identify typical linguistic realizations of these structural elements. We will illustrate this with the example definition given in (3):

(3) [$_4$ Bei einem Einfamilienreihenhaus] [$_3$ liegt] ein [$_1$ mangelhafter Schallschutz] [$_5$ dann] [$_3$ vor, wenn] [$_2$ die Haustrennwand einschalig errichtet wurde] (...).

(One-family row-houses have insufficient noise insulation if the separating wall is one-layered.)

This definition contains:

1. The *definiendum*, i.e. the element that is defined (*unzureichender Schallschutz - insufficient noise insulation*).

2. The *definiens*, i.e. the element that fixes the meaning to be given to the definiendum (*die Haustrennwand einschalig errichtet wurde - the separating wall is one-layered*).

Apart from these constitutive parts, it contains:

3. A *connector*, indicating the relation between definiendum and definiens (*liegt...vor, wenn, have..., if*).

4. A qualification specifying a *domain area* of applicability, i.e. a restriction in terms of the part of reality that the regulation refers to (*bei Einfamilienreihenhäusern - one-family row-houses*).

5. *Signal* words that cannot be assigned any clear function with regard to the content of the sentence, but serve to mark it as a definition (*dann - ø*).

The connector normally contains at least the predicate of the main clause, often together with further material (subjunction, relative pronoun, determiner). It not only indicates the presence of a definition. It also determines how definiens and definiendum are realized linguistically and often contains information about the type of the given definition (full, partial, by examples...). The linguistic realization of definiendum and definiens depends on the connector. One common pattern realizes the definiendum as the subject, and the definiens within a subclause. The domain area is often specified by a PP introduced by *bei ("in the field of", for)*, as seen in the example. Further possibilities are other PPs or certain subclauses. Signal words are certain particles (*dann* in the example), adverbs *(e.g. begrifflich - conceptually*) or nominal constructions containing the definiendum (e.g. *der Begriff des..., the concept of...*).

Of course many definitions also contain further structural elements that are not present in Example (3). For instance certain adverbials or modal verbs modify the force, validity or degree of commitment to a definition (e.g. only for typical cases). The *field of law* within which the given definition applies is often specified as a PP containing a formal reference to sections of statutes or simply the name of a statute, document, or even a complete legal field *(e.g. Umweltrecht - environmental law*). Citation information for definitions is standardly included in brackets as a reference to another verdict by date, court, and reference number.

4 Automatic extraction of definitions

The corpus based pilot study discussed in the last section has on the one hand shown a broad linguistic variation among definitions in reasons for judgement. No simple account, for instance in terms of keyword spotting or pattern matching, will suffice to extract the relevant information from a significant amount of occurrences. On the other hand our survey has shown a range of structural uniformities across these formulations. This section discusses computational linguistic analysis techniques that are useful to identify and segment definitions based on these uniformities.

4.1 Linguistic Analysis

Our current work is based on a collection of more than 6000 verdicts in environmental law that were parsed using the *Preds*-parser (*Preds* stands for *partially resolved dependency structure*), a semantically-oriented parsing system that has been developed in the Saarbrücken Computational Linguistics Department within the project COLLATE. It was used there for information extraction from newspaper text (Braun 2003, Fliedner 2004). The *Preds*-parser balances depth of linguistic analysis with robustness of the analysis process and is therefore able to provide relatively detailed linguistic information even for large amounts of syntactically complex text.

It generates a semantic representation for its input by a cascade of analysis components. Starting with a topological analysis of the input sentence, it continues by applying a phrase chunker and a named entity recognizer to the contents of the topological fields. The resulting extended topological structure is transformed to a semantic representation (called *Preds*, see above) by a series of heuristic rules. The *Preds*-format encodes semantic dependencies and modification relations within a sentence using abstract categories

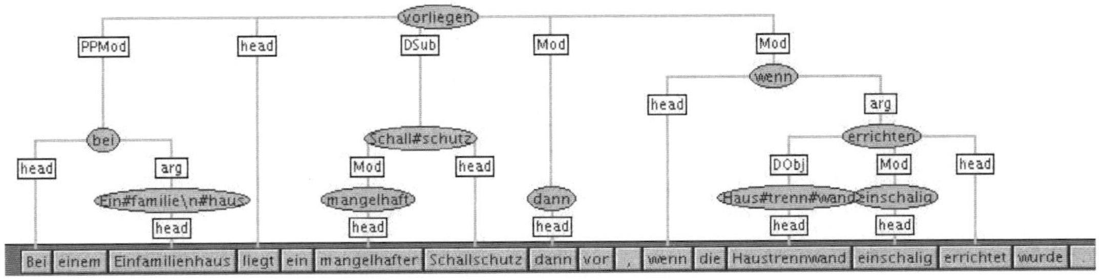

Figure 1. Grammatical structure for Example (3).

such as deep subject and deep object. This way it provides a common normalized structure for various surface realizations of the same content (e.g. in active or passive voice).

The *Preds*-parser makes use of syntactic underspecification to deal with the problem of ambiguity. It systematically prefers low attachment in case of doubt and marks the affected parts of the result as default-based. Later processing steps are enabled to resolve ambiguities based on further information. But this is not necessary in general. Common parts of multiple readings can be accessed without having to enumerate and search through alternative representations. Figure 1 shows the parse for the definition in Example (3).[2] The parser returns an XML-tree that contains this structure together with the full linguistic information accumulated during the analysis process.

4.2 Search and processing

The structures produced by the Preds parser provide a level of abstraction that allows us to turn typical definition patterns into declarative extraction rules. Figure 2 shows one such extraction rule. It specifies (abbreviated) XPath-expressions describing definitions such as Example (3). The field *query* contains an expression characterising a sentence with the predicate *vorliegen* and a subclause that is introduced by the subjunction *wenn (if)*. This expression is evaluated on the *Preds* of the sentences within our corpus to identify definitions. Other fields determine the locations containing the structural elements (such as *definiendum*, *definiens* and domain *area*) within the *Preds* of the identified definitions.

```
<pattern>
description=liegt vor + wenn-Nebensatz
query=sent/parse/preds/word[@stem="vorliegen"
        and INDPRES and WENN]
filters=definite
definiendum=DSub
definiens=WENN/arg/word
area=PPMOD{PREP%bei}
</pattern>
```

Figure 2. Extraction rule.

The field *filters* specifies a set of XSLT-scripts used to filter out certain results. In the example we exclude definienda that are either pronominal (because we do not presently resolve anaphoric references) or definite (because these are often also anaphoric, or indicate that the sentence at hand is valid for that particular case only). Figure 3 shows how the definition in Example (3) is analyzed by this rule.

4.3 Evaluation

We currently use 33 such extraction rules based on the connectors identified in our pilot study, together with various kinds of filters. When applied to the reasons for judgement in all 6000 decisions (containing 237935 sentences) in our environmental law corpus, these rules yield 5461 hits before filtering (since not all patterns are mutually exclusive, these hits are all within 4716 sentences). After exclusion of pronominal and in some cases definite definienda (see above), as well as definienda containing stopwords (certain very common adjectives and nouns) the number of remaining hits decreases to 1486 (in 1342 sentences).

A selection of 492 hits (in 473 sentences; all hits for rules with less than 20, at least 20 hits for others) was checked for precision by two annotators. The evaluation was based on a very inclusive concept of definition, covering many cases of doubt such as negative applicability conditions, legal preconditions or elaborations on the use of evaluative terms. Clear "no"-judgements

[2] Figure 1 and Figure 3 were generated using the SALSA-Tool (Burchardt et al. 2006)

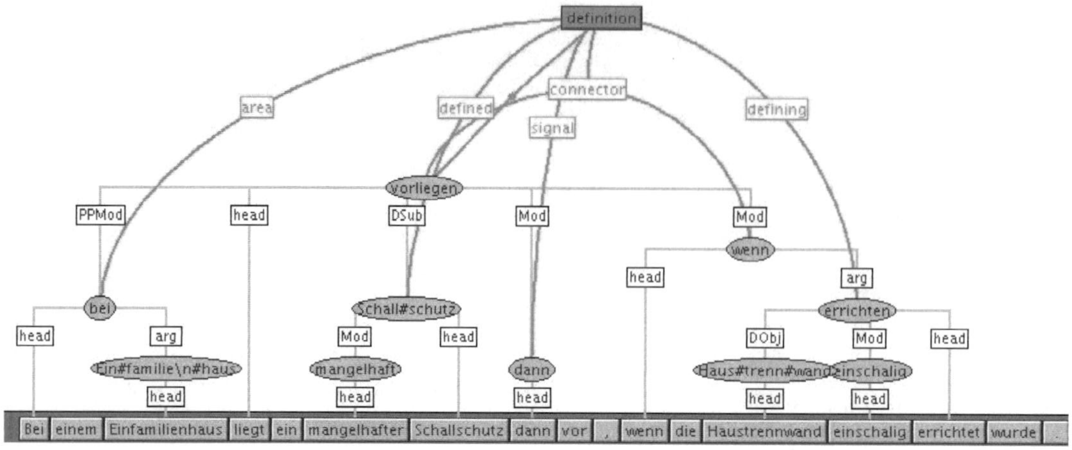

Figure 3. Structural elements of the definition in Example (3).

were e.g. given for statements referring only to one particular case without any general elements, and for purely contingent statements. The overall agreement of the judgements given was relatively high, with an overall κ of 0.835.

Total	
33 rules	1486 hits (1342 / 237935 sent)
Annotator 1	Good: 211/473 (p = 44.6 %)
Annotator 2	Good: 230/473 (p = 48.6 %)
Best rules only	
	Annotator 1
17 rules	749 hits (749 / 1342 sent)
	Good: 176/245 (p = 71.8 %)
	Annotator 2
18 rules	764 hits (633 / 1342 sent)
	Good: 173/230 (p = 75.2 %)

Table 1. Annotation results.

Precision values within the checked hits vary considerably. However in both cases more than 50 % of all hits are by patterns that together still reach a precision of well above 70 % (Table 1).

4.4 Discussion

So far, our focus in selecting rules and filters has been on optimizing precision. As our present results show, it is possible to extract definitions at an interesting degree of precision and still achieve a reasonable number of hits. However we have not addressed the issue of recall systematically yet. The assessment of recall poses greater difficulties than the evaluation of the precision of search patterns. To our knowledge no reference corpus with annotated definitions exists. Building up such a corpus is time intensive, in particular because of the large amount of text that has to be examined for this purpose. Within the 3500 sentences of the 40 decisions examined in our pilot study mentioned above, we found only about 130 definitions. While this amount is significant from the perspective of information access, it is quite small from the annotator's point of view. Moreover it has become clear in our pilot study that there is a considerable amount of definitions that cannot be identified by purely linguistic features, and that many of these are unclear cases of particular difficulty for the annotator. The proportion of such problematic cases will obviously be much higher in free text annotation than in the evaluation of our extraction results, which were generated by looking for clear linguistic cues.

Taking the ratio observed in our pilot study (130 definitions in 3500 sentences) as an orientation, the set of rules we are currently using is clearly far from optimal in terms of recall. It seems that a lot of relatively simple improvements can be made in this respect. A variety of obvious good patterns are still missing in our working set. We are currently testing a bootstrapping approach based on a seed of various noun-combinations taken from extracted definitions in order to acquire further extraction patterns. We hope to be able to iterate this procedure in a process of mutual bootstrapping similar to that described in (Riloff and Jones 1999).

Moreover all presently employed rules use patterns that correspond to the connector-parts (cf. Section 3) of definitions. Accumulations of e.g. certain *signals* and *modifiers* may turn out to indicate definitions with equal precision. We identified a range of adverbial modifiers that are highly associated with definitions in the corpus of our pilot study, but we have not yet evaluated the effect of integrating them in our extraction patterns.

We also assume that there is great potential for more fine-grained and linguistically sensitive filtering, such that comparable precision is achieved without losing so many results.

Even with all of the discussed improvements however, the problem of definitions without clear linguistic indicators will remain. Heuristics based on domain specific information, such as citation and document structure (e.g. the first sentence of a paragraph is often a definition), may be of additional help in extending recall of our method to such cases.

Apart from integrating further features in our extractors and using bootstrapping techniques for identifying new patterns, another option is to train classifiers for the identification of definitions based on parse features, such as dependency paths. This approach has for instance been used successfully for hypernym discovery (cf. Snow et al., 2005). For this task, WordNet could be used as a reference in the training and evaluation phase. The fact that no comparable reference resource is available in our case presents a great difficulty for the application of machine learning methods.

5 Ontology Extraction

Occurrence of a concept within a definition is likely to indicate that the concept is important for the text at hand. Moreover in court decisions, a great deal of the important (legal as well as subject domain) concepts will in fact have at least some occurrences within definitions. This can be assumed because legal argumentation (as discussed in Section 2) characteristically proceeds by adducing explicit definitions for all relevant concepts. Definition extraction therefore seems to be a promising step for identifying concepts, in particular within legal text. This section discusses how extracted definitions can be used to improve the quality of text-based ontology learning from court decisions. For this purpose we first examine the results of a standard method – identification of terms and potential class-subclass-relations through weighted bigrams – and then look at the effect of combining this method with a filter based on occurrence within definitions.

5.1 Bigram Extraction

Adjective-noun-bigrams are often taken as a starting point in text based ontology extraction because in many cases they contain two concepts and one relation (see e.g. Buitelaar et al. 2004). The nominal head represents one concept, while adjective and noun together represent another concept that is subordinate to the first one. There are however obvious limits to the applicability of this *concept-subconcept-rule*:

(1) It may happen that the bigram or even already the nominal head on its own do not correspond to relevant concepts, i.e. that one or both of the denoted classes are of no particular relevance for the domain.

(2) Not all adjective-noun-bigrams refer to a subclass of the class denoted by the head noun. Adjectives may e.g. be used redundantly, making explicit a part of the semantics of the head noun, or the combination may be non-compositional and therefore relatively unrelated to the class referred to by the head noun.

For these reasons, extracted bigrams generally need to be hand-checked before corresponding concepts can be integrated into an ontology. This time-intensive step can be facilitated by providing a relevance-ranking of the candidates to be inspected. Such rankings use association measures known from collocation discovery (like χ^2, pointwise mutual information or log-likelihood-ratios). But while the elements of a collocation are normally associated in virtue of their meaning, they do not necessarily correspond to a domain concept just by this fact. Moreover, many collocations are non-compositional. An association based ranking therefore cannot solve Problem (2) just mentioned, and only partially solves Problem (1). However it seems likely that the definiendum in a definition is a domain concept, and for the reasons discussed in Section 2, it can be assumed that particularly many concepts will in fact occur within definitions in the legal domain. In order to investigate this hypothesis, we extracted all head-modifier pairs with nominal head and adjectival modifier from all parsed sentences in our corpus. We then restricted this list to only those bigrams occurring within at least one identified definiendum, and compared the proportion of domain concepts following the concept-subconcept-rule on both lists.

5.2 Unfiltered Extraction and Annotation

We found a total 165422 bigram-occurrences of 73319 types (in the following we use *bigrams* to refer to types, not to occurrences) within the full corpus. From this list we deleted combinations with 53 very frequent adjectives that are mainly used to establish uniqueness for definite reference (such as *vorgenannt – mentioned above*). All types with more than 5 occurrences were then ranked by log-likelihood of observed compared to independent occurrence of the bigram elements.[3] The resulting list contains 4371 bigrams on 4320 ranks. Each bigram on the first 600 ranks of this list (601 bigrams, two bigrams share rank 529) was assigned one of the following five categories:

1. Environmental domain: Bigrams encoding concepts from the environmental domain (e.g. *unsorted construction waste*). These occur because our corpus deals with environmental law.

2. Legal domain: Bigrams encoding concepts from the legal domain. These range from concepts that are more or less characteristic of environmental law (e.g. various kinds of *town-planning schemes*) to very generic legal concepts (such as *statutory prerequisite*)

3. No subconcept: Bigrams that would be categorized as 1. or 2., but (typically for one of the reasons explained above) do not encode a subconcept of the concept associated with the head noun. An example is *öffentliche Hand* (*"public hand"*, i.e. public authorities – a non-compositional collocation).

4. No concept: All bigrams that - as a bigram - do not stand for a domain concept (although the nominal head alone may stand for a concept).

5. Parser error: Bigrams that were obviously misanalysed due to parser errors.

Figure 4 shows the distribution of categories among the 600 top-ranked bigrams, as well as within an additionally annotated 100 ranks towards the end of the list (ranks 3400-3500).

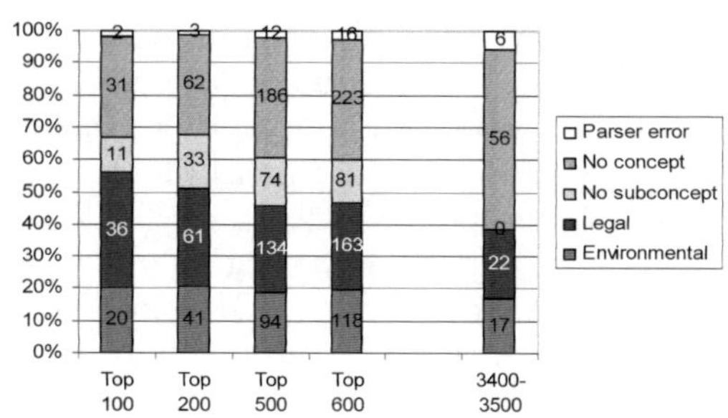

Figure 4. Results of log-likelihood ranking.

[3] The ranking was calculated by the Ngram Statistics Package described in (Bannerjee and Pedersen 2003)

For selecting the two categories of central interest, namely those of legal and environmental concepts to which the concept-subconcept rule applies, the ranking is most precise on the first few hundred ranks, and looses much of its effect on lower ranks. The percentage of such concepts decreases from 56% among the first 100 ranks to 51% among the first 200, but is roughly the same within the first 500 and 600 ranks (with even a slight increase, 45.6% compared to 46.8%). Even the segment from rank 3400 to 3500 still contains 39% of relevant terminology. There are no bigrams of the "no subconcept" category within this final segment. The explanation for this fact is probably that such bigrams (especially the non-compositional ones) are mostly established collocations and therefore show a particularly high degree of association.

It must be noted that the results of our annotation have to be interpreted cautiously. They have not yet been double-checked and during the annotation process there turned out to be a certain degree of uncertainty especially in the subclassification of the various categories of concepts (1, 2 and 3). A further category for concepts with generic attributes (e.g. *permissible*, combining with a whole range of one-word terms) would probably cover many cases of doubt. The binary distinction between concepts and non-concepts in contrast was less difficult to make, and it is surely safe to conclude about general tendencies based on our annotation.

5.3 Filtering and Combined Approach

By selecting only those bigrams that occur within defienda, the 4371 items on the original list were were reduced to 227 (to allow for comparison, these were kept in the same order and annotated with their ranks as on the original list). Figure 5 shows how the various categories are distributed within the items selected from the top segments of the original list, as well as within the complete 227 filtering results.

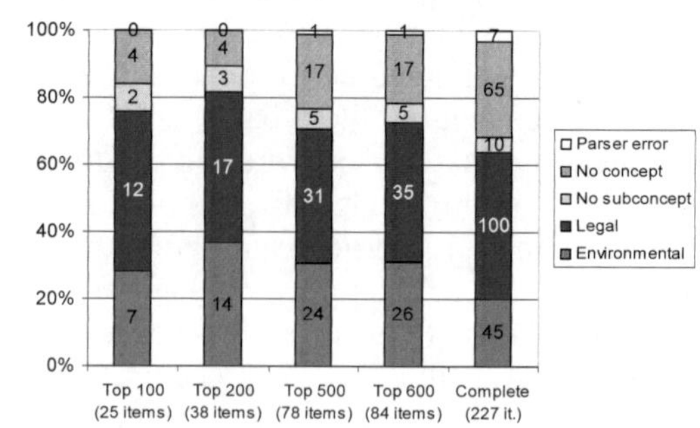

Figure 5. Filtered results

The proportion of interesting concepts reaches about 80% and is higher than 60% on the complete selection. This is still well above the 56% precision within the top 100-segment of the original list. However the restriction to a total of 227 results on our filtered list (of which only 145 are useful) means a dramatic loss in recall. This problem can be alleviated by leaving a top segment of the original list in place (e.g. the top 200 or 500 ranks, where precision is still at a tolerably high level) and supplementing it with the lower ranks from the filtered list until the desired number of items is reached. Another option is to apply the filtering to the complete list of extracted bigrams, not only to those that occur more than 5 times. We assume that a concept that is explicitly defined is likely to be of particular relevance for the domain regardless of its frequency. Hence our definition-based filter should still work well on concept candidates that are too infrequent to be considered at all in a log-likelihood ranking, and allow us to include such candidates in our selection, too.

We investigated the effect of a combination of both methods just described. For this purpose, we first extracted all noun-adjective bigrams occurring within any of the identified definienda, regardless of their frequency within the corpus. After completing the annotation on the 627 resulting bigrams they were combined with various top segments of our original unfiltered list.

Figure 6 shows the distribution of the annotated categories among the 627 bigrams from definienda, as well as on two combined lists. *Cutoff 200/750* is the result of cutting the original list at rank 200 and filling up with the next 550 items from the filtered list. For *cutoff 500/1000* we cut the original list at rank 500 and filled up with the following 500 items from the filtered one. The distribution of categories among the original top 200 is repeated for comparison.

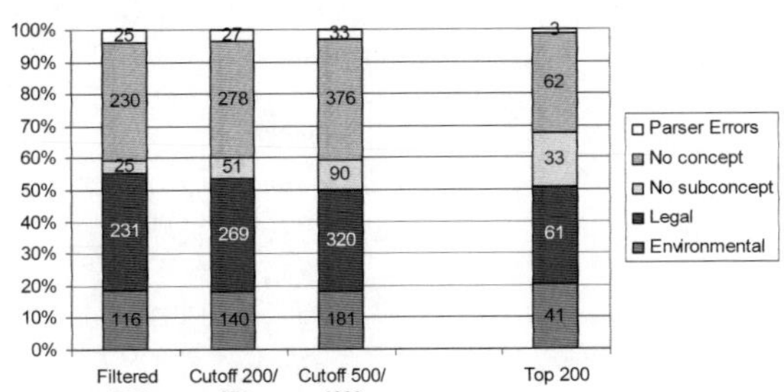

Figure 6. Log-likelihood and filtering combined.

Precision among the 627 filtering results is higher than among the original top 200 (almost 56% compared to 51%), and only slightly smaller even for the 1000 results in the *cutoff 500/1000* setting. Using definition extraction as an additional knowledge source, the top 1000 results retrieved are thus of a quality that can otherwise only be achieved for the top 200 results.

6 Conclusion

In this paper we argued that definitions are an important element of legal texts and in particular of court decisions. We provided a structural segmentation scheme for definitions and discussed a method of applying computational linguistic analysis techniques for their text-based extraction and automatic segmentation. We showed that a large number of definitions can in fact be extracted at high precision using this method, but we also pointed out that there is still much room for improvement in terms of recall, e.g. through the inclusion of further definition patterns.

Our future work in this area will focus on the integration of extraction results across documents (e.g. recognizing and collecting complementary definitions for the same concept) and on a user interface for structured access to this data. For this work we have access to a corpus of several million verdicts provided to us by the company *juris GmbH,* Saarbrücken. We also demonstrated how the identification of definitions can improve the results of text-driven ontology learning in the legal domain. When looking for noun-adjective bigrams encoding relevant concepts, it leads to a considerable increase in precision to restrict the search to definienda only. This method is more precise than selecting the top ranks of a log-likelihood ranking. Its great disadvantage is the very low total number of results, leading to poor recall. However by combining a log-likelihood ranking with definition-based concept extraction, recall can be improved while still achieving better precision than with a log-likelihood ranking alone. Moreover this combined method also retrieves concepts that are too infrequent to be included at all in a log-likelihood ranking.

There is however another, maybe even more relevant reason to look for definitions in ontology learning. Definitions in legal text often very explicitly and precisely determine all kinds of relational knowledge about the defined concept. For instance they specify explicit subordinations (as in the classical *definitio per genus et differen-*

tiam), introduce restrictions on roles inherited from a superconcept, determine the constitutive parts of the definiendum, or contain information about its causal relations to other concepts. As one focus of our future work we plan to investigate how such rich ontological knowledge can be extracted automatically.

References

Satanjeev Banerjee and Ted Pedersen. 2003. The Design, Implementation, and Use of the Ngram Statistics Package. *CICLing 2003*: 370-381

Christian Braun. 2003. Parsing German text for syntacto-semantic structures. In *Prospects and Advances in the Syntax/Semantics Interface*, Lorraine-Saarland Workshop Series, Nancy, France:99-102

Paul Buitelaar, Daniel Olejnik, Michael Sintek. 2004. A Protégé Plug-In for Ontology Extraction from Text Based on Linguistic Analysis In: *Proceedings of the 1st European Semantic Web Symposium (ESWS)*, Heraklion, Greece

Aljoscha Burchardt, Katrin Erk, Anette Frank, Andrea Kowalski and Sebastian Padó. 2006. SALTO -- A Versatile Multi-Level Annotation Tool. *Proceedings of LREC 2006*, Genoa, Italy.

Gerhard Fliedner. 2004. Deriving FrameNet Representations: Towards Meaning-Oriented Question Answering. *Proceedings of the International Conference on Applications of Natural Language to Information Systems (NLDB).* Salford, UK. LNCS 3136/2004. Springer. 64–75.

Herbert L.A. Hart. 1961. *The concept of Law*. Oxford University Press, London, UK

Guiraude Lame. 2005. Using NLP Techniques to Identify Legal Ontology Components: Concepts and Relations, *Lecture Notes in Computer Science, Volume 3369*:169 – 184

Ellen Riloff and Rosie Jones. 1999. Learning Dictionaries for Information Extraction Using Multi-level Boot-strapping, *Proceedings of AAAI-99*, 474 - 479

José Saias and Paulo Quaresma. 2005. A Methodology to Create Legal Ontologies in a Logic Programming Information Retrieval System. *Lecture Notes in Computer Science, Volume 3369*:185 - 200

Rion Snow, Daniel Jurafsky, and Andrew Y. Ng. 2005. Learning syntactic patterns for automatic hypernym discovery, *Proceedings of NIPS 2004,* Vancouver, Canada.

Andre Valente. 2005. Types and Roles of Legal Ontologies. *Lecture Notes in Computer Science, Volume 3369*:65 - 76.

Andre Valente and Jost Breuker. 1994. A functional ontology of law. *Towards a global expert system in law.* CEDAM Publishers, Padua, Italy

Improving Semi-Supervised Acquisition of Relation Extraction Patterns

Mark A. Greenwood and Mark Stevenson
Department of Computer Science
University of Sheffield
Sheffield, S1 4DP, UK
{m.greenwood,marks}@dcs.shef.ac.uk

Abstract

This paper presents a novel approach to the semi-supervised learning of Information Extraction patterns. The method makes use of more complex patterns than previous approaches and determines their similarity using a measure inspired by recent work using kernel methods (Culotta and Sorensen, 2004). Experiments show that the proposed similarity measure outperforms a previously reported measure based on cosine similarity when used to perform binary relation extraction.

1 Introduction

A recent approach to Information Extraction (IE) is to make use of machine learning algorithms which allow systems to be rapidly developed or adapted to new extraction problems. This reduces the need for manual development which is a major bottleneck in the development of IE technologies and can be extremely time consuming (e.g. Riloff (1996)).

A number of machine learning approaches have recently been applied. One is the use of iterative learning algorithms to infer extraction patterns from a small number of seed examples (Yangarber et al., 2000; Stevenson and Greenwood, 2005). These approaches use dependency analysis as the basis of IE patterns. Training text is parsed and a set of candidate patterns extracted. These patterns are then compared against the seeds with the most similar being selected and added to the seed set. (Optionally, a user may verify the patterns at this point.) The process is then repeated with the remaining patterns being compared to the enlarged seed set. The process continues until a suitable set of patterns has been learned. These approaches require only a small number of example extraction patterns which greatly reduces the effort required to develop IE systems.

While it has been found that these approaches are capable of learning useful IE patterns from a handful of examples (Yangarber et al., 2000; Stevenson and Greenwood, 2005) they are limited by the use of basic extraction patterns: SVO tuples. The patterns used by these systems are defined as a verb and its direct subject and/or object. They could then only extract a limited set of relations; those expressed using a verb and its direct arguments. For example, these patterns could identify the relation between *Jones* and *Smith* in the sentence *"Jones replaced Smith"*. However, no pattern consisting of a verb and its arguments could be constructed which could identify the same relation in *"Jones was named as Smith's successor."*

Others have suggested alternative approaches for generating extraction patterns from dependency trees, each of which allows a particular part of the dependency analysis to act as an extraction pattern. For example, Sudo et al. (2003) used patterns consisting of a path from a verb to any of its descendents (direct or indirect) while Bunescu and Mooney (2005) suggest the shortest path between the items being related. However, iterative learning algorithms, such as the ones used by Yangarber et al. (2000) and Stevenson and Greenwood (2005), have not made use of these more complex extraction patterns. Part of the reason for this is that these algorithms require a way of determining the similarity between patterns (in order to compare candidate patterns with the seeds). This process is straightforward for simple patterns, based on SVO tuples, but less so for more complex ex-

Proceedings of the Workshop on Information Extraction Beyond The Document, pages 29–35,
Sydney, July 2006.

traction patterns.

In this paper we present a semi-supervised algorithm for the iterative learning of relation extraction patterns which makes use of a more complex pattern representation than has been previously used by these approaches (Sections 2 and 3). The algorithm makes use of a similarity function based on those which have been proposed for use with non-iterative learning algorithms (Zelenko et al., 2003; Culotta and Sorensen, 2004; Bunescu and Mooney, 2005). These are extended to include information about lexical similarity derived from WordNet (Section 4). We present results of using patterns acquired through this similarity function to perform binary relation extraction (Sections 5 and 6).

2 Semi-Supervised Learning of Extraction Patterns

We begin by outlining the general process of learning extraction patterns using a semi-supervised algorithm, similar to one presented by Yangarber (2003).

1. For a given IE scenario we assume the existence of a set of documents against which the system can be trained. The documents are unannotated and may be either relevant (contain the description of an event relevant to the scenario) or irrelevant.
2. This corpus is pre-processed to generate a set of all patterns which could be used to represent sentences contained in the corpus, call this set P. The aim of the learning process is to identify the subset of P representing patterns which are relevant to the IE scenario.
3. The user provides a small set of seed patterns, P_{seed}, which are relevant to the scenario. These patterns are used to form the set of currently accepted patterns, P_{acc}, so $P_{acc} \leftarrow P_{seed}$. The remaining patterns are treated as candidates for inclusion in the accepted set, these form the set $P_{cand}(= P - P_{acc})$.
4. A function, f, is used to assign a score to each pattern in P_{cand} based on those which are currently in P_{acc}. This function assigns a real number to candidate patterns so $\forall\, c \in P_{cand},\ f(c, P_{acc}) \mapsto \mathbb{R}$. A set of high scoring patterns (based on absolute scores or ranks after the set of patterns has been ordered by scores) are chosen as being suitable for inclusion in the set of accepted patterns. These form the set P_{learn}.
5. (Optional) The patterns in P_{learn} may be reviewed by a user who may remove any they do not believe to be useful for the scenario.
6. The patterns in P_{learn} are added to P_{acc} and removed from P_{cand}, so $P_{acc} \leftarrow P_{acc} \cup P_{learn}$ and $P_{cand} \leftarrow P_{acc} - P_{learn}$
7. Stop if an acceptable set of patterns has been learned, otherwise goto step 4

Previous algorithms which use this approach include those described by Yangarber et al. (2000) and Stevenson and Greenwood (2005). A key choice in the development of an algorithm using this approach is the process of ranking candidate patterns (step 4) since this determines the patterns which will be learned at each iteration. Yangarber et al. (2000) chose an approach motivated by the assumption that documents containing a large number of patterns already identified as relevant to a particular IE scenario are likely to contain further relevant patterns. This approach operates by associating confidence scores with patterns and relevance scores with documents. Initially seed patterns are given a maximum confidence score of 1 and all others a 0 score. Each document is given a relevance score based on the patterns which occur within it. Candidate patterns are ranked according to the proportion of relevant and irrelevant documents in which they occur, those found in relevant documents far more than in irrelevant ones are ranked highly. After new patterns have been accepted all patterns' confidence scores are updated, based on the documents in which they occur, and documents' relevance according to the accepted patterns they contain.

Stevenson and Greenwood (2005) suggested an alternative method for ranking the candidate patterns. Their approach relied on the assumption that useful patterns will have similar meanings to the patterns which have already been accepted. They chose to represent each pattern as a vector consisting of the lexical items which formed the pattern and used a version of the cosine metric to determine the similarity between pairs of patterns, consequently this approach is referred to as "cosine similarity". The metric used by this approach incorporated information from WordNet and assigned high similarity scores to patterns with similar meanings expressed in different ways.

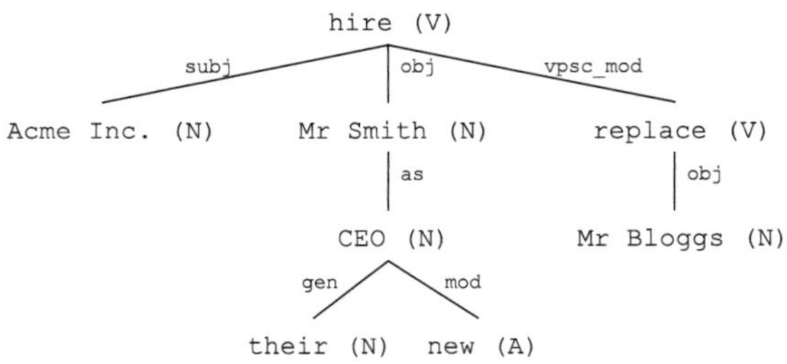

Figure 1: An example dependency tree.

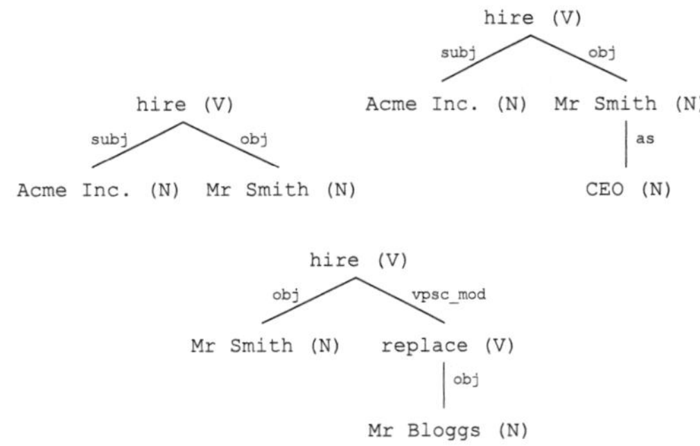

Figure 2: Example linked chain patterns

3 Relation Extraction Patterns

Both these approaches used extraction patterns which were based on dependency analysis (Tesniére, 1959) of text. Under this approach the structure of a sentence is represented by a set of directed binary links between a word (the head) and one of its modifiers. These links may be labelled to indicate the grammatical relation between the head and modifier (e.g. subject, object). Cyclical paths are generally disallowed and the analysis forms a tree structure. An example dependency analysis for the sentence *"Acme Inc. hired Mr Smith as their new CEO, replacing Mr Bloggs."* is shown in Figure 1.

The extraction patterns used by both Yangarber et al. (2000) and Stevenson and Greenwood (2005) were based on SVO tuples extracted from dependency trees. The dependency tree shown in Figure 1 would generate two patterns: `replace` $\xrightarrow{obj}$ `Mr Bloggs` and `Acme Inc.` $\xleftarrow{subj}$ `hire` $\xrightarrow{obj}$ `Mr Smith`. While these represent some of the core information in this sentence, they cannot be used to identify a number of relations including the connection between *Mr. Smith* and *CEO* or between *Mr. Smith* and *Mr. Bloggs*.

A number of alternative approaches to constructing extraction patterns from dependency trees have been proposed (e.g. (Sudo et al., 2003; Bunescu and Mooney, 2005)). Previous analysis (Stevenson and Greenwood, 2006a) suggests that the most useful of these is one based on pairs of linked chains from the dependency tree. A chain can be defined as a path between a verb node and any other node in the dependency tree passing through zero or more intermediate nodes (Sudo et al., 2001). The linked chains model (Greenwood et al., 2005) represents extraction patterns as a pair of chains which share the same verb but no direct descendants. It can be shown that linked chain patterns can represent the majority of relations within a dependency analysis (Stevenson and Greenwood, 2006a). For example, the dependency tree shown in Figure 1 contains four named entities (*Acme Inc.*, *Mr Smith*, *CEO* and *Mr. Bloggs*) and linked chains patterns can be used to represent the relation between any pair.[1] Some example patterns extracted from the analysis in Figure 1 can be seen in Figure 2. An additional advantage of linked chain patterns is that they do not cause an unwieldy number of candidate patterns to be generated unlike some other approaches for representing extraction patterns, such as the one proposed by Sudo et al. (2003) where any subtree of the dependency tree can act as a potential pattern.

When used within IE systems these patterns are generalised by replacing terms which refer to specific entities with a general semantic class. For example, the pattern `Acme Inc.` $\xleftarrow{subj}$ `hire` $\xrightarrow{obj}$ `Mr Smith` would become `COMPANY` $\xleftarrow{subj}$ `hire` $\xrightarrow{obj}$ `PERSON`.

4 Pattern Similarity

Patterns such as linked chains have not been used by semi-supervised approaches to pattern learning. These algorithms require a method of determining the similarity of patterns. Simple patterns, such as SVO tuples, have a fixed structure containing few items and tend to occur relatively frequently in corpora. However, more complex patterns, such as linked chains, have a less fixed structure and occur less frequently. Consequently, the previously proposed approaches for determining pattern similarity (see Section 2) are unlikely to be as successful with these more complex patterns. The approach proposed by Stevenson and

[1] Note that we allow a linked chain pattern to represent the relation between two items when they are on the same chain, such as *Mr Smith* and *CEO* in this example.

Greenwood (2005) relies on representing patterns as vectors which is appropriate for SVO tuples but not when patterns may include significant portions of the dependency tree. Yangarber et al. (2000) suggested a method where patterns were compared based on their distribution across documents in a corpus. However, since more complex patterns are more specific they occur with fewer corpus instances which is likely to hamper this type of approach.

Another approach to relation extraction is to use supervised learning algorithms, although they require more training data than semi-supervised approaches. In particular various approaches (Zelenko et al., 2003; Culotta and Sorensen, 2004; Bunescu and Mooney, 2005) have used kernel methods to determine the sentences in a corpus which contain instances of a particular relation. Kernel methods (Vapnik, 1998) allow the representation of large and complicated feature spaces and are therefore suitable when the instances are complex extraction rules, such as linked chains. Several previous kernels used for relation extraction have been based on trees and include methods based on shallow parse trees (Zelenko et al., 2003), dependency trees (Culotta and Sorensen, 2004) and part of a dependency tree which represents the shortest path between the items being related (Bunescu and Mooney, 2005). Kernels methods rely on a similarity function between pairs of instances (the kernel) and these can be used within semi-supervised approaches to pattern learning such as those outlined in Section 2.

4.1 Structural Similarity Measure

The remainder of this Section describes a similarity function for pairs of linked chains, based on the tree kernel proposed by Culotta and Sorensen (2004). The measure compares patterns by following their structure from the root nodes through the patterns until they diverge too far to be considered similar.

Each node in an extraction pattern has three features associated with it: the word, the relation to a parent, and the part-of-speech (POS) tag. The values of these features for node n are denoted by n_{word}, n_{reln} and n_{pos} respectively. Pairs of nodes can be compared by examining the values of these features and also by determining the semantic similarity of the words. A set of four functions, $F = \{word, relation, pos, semantic\}$, is used to compare nodes. The first three of these correspond to the node features with the same name; the relevant function returns 1 if the value of the feature is equal for the two nodes and 0 otherwise. For example, the pos function compares the values of the part of speech feature for nodes n_1 and n_2:

$$pos\,(n_1, n_2) = \begin{cases} 1 & \text{if } n_1, pos = n_2, pos \\ 0 & otherwise \end{cases}$$

The remaining function, $semantic$, returns a value between 0 and 1 to signify the semantic similarity of lexical items contained in the word feature of each node. This similarity is computed using the WordNet (Fellbaum, 1998) similarity function introduced by Lin (1998) .

The similarity of two nodes is zero if their part of speech tags are different and, otherwise, is simply the sum of the scores provided by the four functions which form the set F. This is represented by the function s:

$$s\,(n_1, n_2) = \begin{cases} 0 \text{ if } pos(n_1, n_2) = 0 \\ \sum_{f \in F} f\,(n_1, n_2) \text{ otherwise} \end{cases}$$

The similarity of a pair of linked chain patterns, l_1 and l_2, is determined by the function sim:

$$sim\,(l_1, l_2) = \begin{cases} 0 \text{ if } s\,(r_1, r_2) = 0 \\ s\,(r_1, r_2) + \\ sim_c\,(C_{r_1}, C_{r_2}) \text{ otherwise} \end{cases}$$

where r_1 and r_2 are the root nodes of patterns l_1 and l_2 (respectively) and C_r is the set of children of node r.

The final part of the similarity function calculates the similarity between the child nodes of n_1 and n_2.[2]

$$sim_c\,(C_{n_1}, C_{n_2}) = \sum_{c_1 \in C_{n_1}} \sum_{c_2 \in C_{n_2}} sim\,(c_1, c_2)$$

Using this similarity function a pair of identical nodes have a similarity score of four. Consequently, the similarity score for a pair of linked chain patterns can be normalised by dividing the similarity score by 4 times the size (in nodes) of the larger pattern. This results in a similarity function that is not biased towards either small or large patterns but will select the most similar pattern to those already accepted as representative of the domain.

This similarity function resembles the one introduced by Culotta and Sorensen (2004) but also

[2] In linked chain patterns the only nodes with multiple children are the root nodes so, in all but the first application, this formula can be simplified to $sim_c\,(C_{n_1}, C_{n_2}) = sim(c_1, c_2)$.

differs in a number of ways. Both functions make use of WordNet to compare tree nodes. Culotta and Sorensen (2004) consider whether one node is the hypernym of the other while the approach introduced here makes use of existing techniques to measure semantic similarity. The similarity function introduced by Culotta and Sorensen (2004) compares subsequences of child nodes which is not required for our measure since it is concerned only with linked chain extraction patterns.

5 Experiments

This structural similarity metric was implemented within the general framework for semi-supervised pattern learning presented in Section 2. At each iteration the candidate patterns are compared against the set of currently accepted patterns and ranked according to the average similarity with the set of similar accepted patterns. The four highest scoring patterns are considered for acceptance but a pattern is only accepted if its score is within 0.95 of the similarity of the highest scoring pattern.

We conducted experiments which compared the proposed pattern similarity metric with the vector space approach used by Stevenson and Greenwood (2005) (see Section 2). That approach was originally developed for simple extraction patterns consisting of subject-verb-object tuples but was extended for extraction patterns in the linked chain format by Greenwood et al. (2005). We use the measure developed by Lin (1998) to provide information about lexical similarity. This is the same measure which is used within the structural similarity metric (Section 4).

Three different configurations of the iterative learning algorithm were compared. (1) **Cosine (SVO)** This approach uses the SVO model for extraction patterns and the cosine similarity metric to compare them (see Section 2). This version of the algorithm acts as a baseline which represents previously reported approaches (Stevenson and Greenwood, 2005; Stevenson and Greenwood, 2006b). (2) **Cosine (Linked chain)** uses extraction patterns based on the linked chain model along with the cosine similarity to compare them and is intended to determine the benefit which is gained from using the more expressive patterns. (3) **Structural (Linked chain)** also uses linked chain extraction patterns but compares them using the similarity measure introduced in Section 4.1.

$\texttt{COMPANY}\xleftarrow{subj}\texttt{appoint}\xrightarrow{obj}\texttt{PERSON}$
$\texttt{COMPANY}\xleftarrow{subj}\texttt{elect}\xrightarrow{obj}\texttt{PERSON}$
$\texttt{COMPANY}\xleftarrow{subj}\texttt{promote}\xrightarrow{obj}\texttt{PERSON}$
$\texttt{COMPANY}\xleftarrow{subj}\texttt{name}\xrightarrow{obj}\texttt{PERSON}$
$\texttt{PERSON}\xleftarrow{subj}\texttt{resign}$
$\texttt{PERSON}\xleftarrow{subj}\texttt{depart}$
$\texttt{PERSON}\xleftarrow{subj}\texttt{quit}$

Table 1: Seed patterns used by the learning algorithm

5.1 IE Scenario

Experiments were carried out on the management succession extraction task used for the Sixth Message Understanding Conference (MUC-6) (MUC, 1995). This IE scenario concerns the movement of executives between positions and companies. We used a version of the evaluation data which was produced by Soderland (1999) in which each event was converted into a set of binary asymmetric relations. The corpus contains four types of relation: `Person-Person`, `Person-Post`, `Person-Organisation`, and `Post-Organisation`. At each iteration of the algorithm the related items identified by the current set of learned patterns are extracted from the text and compared against the set of related items which are known to be correct. The systems are evaluated using the widely used precision (P) and recall (R) metrics which are combined using the F-measure (F).

The texts used for these experiments have been previously annotated with named entities. MINIPAR (Lin, 1999), after being adapted to handle the named entity tags, was used to produce the dependency analysis from which the pattersn were generated. All experiments used the seed patterns in Table 1 which are indicative of this extraction task and have been used in previous experiments into semi-supervised IE pattern acquisition (Stevenson and Greenwood, 2005; Yangarber et al., 2000).

The majority of previous semi-supervised approaches to IE have been evaluated over preliminary tasks such as the identification of event participants (Sudo et al., 2003) or sentence filtering (Stevenson and Greenwood, 2005). These may be a useful preliminary tasks but it is not clear to what extent the success of such systems will be repeated when used to perform relation extraction. Conse-

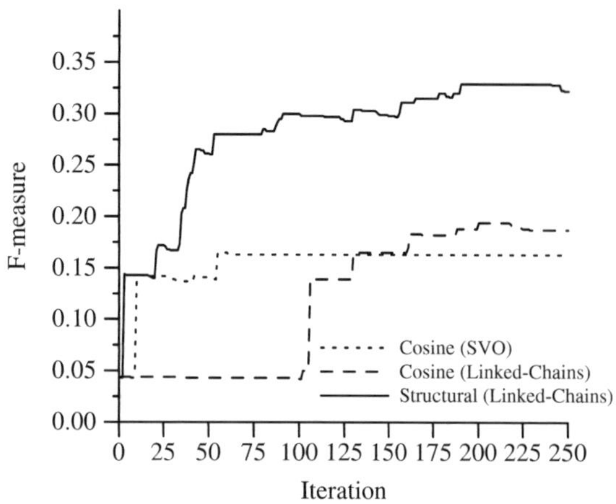

Figure 3: F-measure scores for relation extraction over 250 iterations

quently we chose a relation extraction task to evaluate the work presented here.

6 Results

Results from the relation extraction evaluation can be seen in Table 2 and Figure 3. The seven seed patterns achieve a precision of 0.833 and recall of 0.022. The two approaches based on cosine similarity performs poorly, irrespective of the pattern model being used. The maximum increase in F-measure of 0.15 (when using the cosine measure with the linked chain model) results in a maximum F-measure for the cosine similarity model of 0.194 (with a precision of 0.491 and recall of 0.121) after 200 iterations.

The best result is recorded when the linked chain model is used with the similarity measure introduced in Section 4.1, achieving a maximum F-measure of 0.329 (with a precision of 0.434 and recall of 0.265) after 190 iterations. This is not a high F-measure when compared against supervised IE systems, however it should be remembered that this represents an increase of 0.285 in F-measure over the original seven seed patterns and that this is achieved with a semi-supervised algorithm.

7 Conclusions

A number of conclusions can be drawn from the work described in this paper. Firstly, semi-supervised approaches to IE pattern acquisition benefit from the use of more expressive extraction pattern models since it has been shown that the performance of the linked chain model on the relation extraction task is superior to the simpler SVO model. We have previously presented a theoretical analysis (Stevenson and Greenwood, 2006a) which suggested that the linked chain model was a more suitable format for IE patterns than the SVO model but these experiments are, to our knowledge, the first to show that applying this model improves learning performance. Secondly, these experiments demonstrate that similarity measures inspired by kernel functions developed for use in supervised learning algorithms can be applied to semi-supervised approaches. This suggests that future work in this area should consider applying other similarity functions, including kernel methods, developed for supervised learning algorithms to the task of semi-supervised IE pattern acquisition. Finally, we demonstrated that this similarity measure outperforms a previously proposed approach which was based on cosine similarity and a vector space representation of patterns (Stevenson and Greenwood, 2005).

Acknowledgements

This work was carried out as part of the RESuLT project funded by the Engineering and Physical Sciences Research Council (GR/T06391) and partially funded by the IST 6th Framework project X-Media (FP6-26978).

References

Razvan Bunescu and Raymond Mooney. 2005. A shortest path dependency kernel for relation extraction. In *Proceedings of the Human Language Technology Conference and Conference on Empirical Methods in Natural Language Processing*, pages 724–731, Vancouver, B.C.

Aron Culotta and Jeffery Sorensen. 2004. Dependency Tree Kernels for Relation Extraction. In *42nd Annual Meeting of the Association for Computational Linguistics*, Barcelona, Spain.

Christiane Fellbaum, editor. 1998. *WordNet: An Electronic Lexical Database and some of its Applications*. MIT Press, Cambridge, MA.

Mark A. Greenwood, Mark Stevenson, Yikun Guo, Henk Harkema, and Angus Roberts. 2005. Automatically Acquiring a Linguistically Motivated Genic Interaction Extraction System. In *Proceedings of the 4th Learning Language in Logic Workshop (LLL05)*, Bonn, Germany.

Dekang Lin. 1998. An information-theoretic definition of similarity. In *Proceedings of the Fif-*

Iteration	Cosine (SVO)			Cosine (Linked Chains)			Structural (Linked Chains)		
#	P	R	F	P	R	F	P	R	F
0	0.833	0.022	0.044	0.833	0.022	0.044	0.833	0.022	0.044
25	0.600	0.081	0.142	0.833	0.022	0.044	0.511	0.103	0.172
50	0.380	0.085	0.139	0.500	0.022	0.043	0.482	0.179	0.261
75	0.383	0.103	0.163	0.417	0.022	0.043	0.484	0.197	0.280
100	0.383	0.103	0.163	0.385	0.022	0.042	0.471	0.220	0.300
125	0.383	0.103	0.163	0.500	0.081	0.139	0.441	0.220	0.293
150	0.383	0.103	0.163	0.500	0.099	0.165	0.429	0.229	0.298
175	0.383	0.103	0.163	0.481	0.112	0.182	0.437	0.247	0.315
200	0.383	0.103	0.163	0.491	0.121	0.194	0.434	0.265	0.329
225	0.383	0.103	0.163	0.415	0.121	0.188	0.434	0.265	0.329
250	0.383	0.103	0.163	0.409	0.121	0.187	0.413	0.265	0.322

Table 2: Comparison of the different similarity functions when used to perform relation extraction

teenth International Conference on Machine learning (ICML-98), Madison, Wisconsin.

Dekang Lin. 1999. MINIPAR: A Minimalist Parser. In *Maryland Linguistics Colloquium*, University of Maryland, College Park.

MUC. 1995. *Proceedings of the Sixth Message Understanding Conference (MUC-6)*, San Mateo, CA. Morgan Kaufmann.

Ellen Riloff. 1996. Automatically generating extraction patterns from untagged text. In *Thirteenth National Conference on Artificial Intelligence (AAAI-96)*, pages 1044–1049, Portland, OR.

Stephen Soderland. 1999. Learning Information Extraction Rules for Semi-structured and free text. *Machine Learning*, 31(1-3):233–272.

Mark Stevenson and Mark A. Greenwood. 2005. A Semantic Approach to IE Pattern Induction. In *Proceedings of the 43rd Annual Meeting of the Association for Computational Linguistics*, pages 379–386, Ann Arbor, MI.

Mark Stevenson and Mark A. Greenwood. 2006a. Comparing Information Extraction Pattern Models. In *Proceedings of the Information Extraction Beyond The Document Workshop (COLING/ACL 2006)*, Sydney, Australia.

Mark Stevenson and Mark A. Greenwood. 2006b. Learning Information Extraction Patterns using WordNet. In *Third International Global WordNet Conference (GWC-2006)*, Jeju Island, Korea.

Kiyoshi Sudo, Satoshi Sekine, and Ralph Grishman. 2001. Automatic Pattern Acquisition for Japanese Information Extraction. In *Proceedings of the Human Language Technology Conference (HLT2001)*.

Kiyoshi Sudo, Satoshi Sekine, and Ralph Grishman. 2003. An Improved Extraction Pattern Representation Model for Automatic IE Pattern Acquisition. In *Proceedings of the 41st Annual Meeting of the Association for Computational Linguistics (ACL-03)*, pages 224–231, Sapporo, Japan.

Lucien Tesniére. 1959. *Eleménts de Syntaxe Structurale*. Klincksiek, Paris.

Vladimir Vapnik. 1998. *Statistical Learning Theory*. John Wiley and Sons.

Roman Yangarber, Ralph Grishman, Pasi Tapanainen, and Silja Huttunen. 2000. Automatic Acquisition of Domain Knowledge for Information Extraction. In *Proceedings of the 18th International Conference on Computational Linguistics (COLING 2000)*, pages 940–946, Saarbrücken, Germany.

Roman Yangarber. 2003. Counter-training in the Discovery of Semantic Patterns. In *Proceedings of the 41st Annual Meeting of the Association for Computational Linguistics (ACL 03)*, pages 343–350, Sapporo, Japan.

Dimitry Zelenko, Chinatsu Aone, and Anthony Richardella. 2003. Kernel methods for relation extraction. *Journal of Machine Learning Research*, 3:1083–1106.

Automatic Knowledge Representation using a Graph-based Algorithm for Language-Independent Lexical Chaining

Gaël Dias
HULTIG
University of Beira Interior
Covilhã, Portugal
ddg@di.ubi.pt

Cláudia Santos
HULTIG
University of Beira Interior
Covilhã, Portugal
claudia@dmnet.ubi.pt

Guillaume Cleuziou
LIFO
University of Orléans
Orléans, France
cleuziou@univ-orleans.fr

Abstract

Lexical Chains are powerful representations of documents. In particular, they have successfully been used in the field of Automatic Text Summarization. However, until now, Lexical Chaining algorithms have only been proposed for English. In this paper, we propose a greedy Language-Independent algorithm that automatically extracts Lexical Chains from texts. For that purpose, we build a hierarchical lexico-semantic knowledge base from a collection of texts by using the Pole-Based Overlapping Clustering Algorithm. As a consequence, our methodology can be applied to any language and proposes a solution to language-dependent Lexical Chainers.

1 Introduction

Lexical Chains are powerful representations of documents compared to broadly used bag-of-words representations. In particular, they have successfully been used in the field of Automatic Text Summarization (Barzilay and Elhadad, 1997). However, until now, Lexical Chaining algorithms have only been proposed for English as they rely on linguistic resources such as Thesauri (Morris and Hirst, 1991) or Ontologies (Barzilay and Elhadad, 1997; Hirst and St-Onge, 1997; Silber and McCoy, 2002; Galley and McKeown, 2003).

Morris and Hirst (1991) were the first to propose the concept of Lexical Chains to explore the discourse structure of a text. However, at the time of writing their paper, no machine-readable thesaurus was available so they manually generated Lexical Chains using Roget's Thesaurus (Roget, 1852).

A first computational model of Lexical Chains is introduced by Hirst and St-Onge (1997). Their biggest contribution to the study of Lexical Chains is the mapping of WordNet (Miller, 1995) relations and paths (transitive relationships) to (Morris and Hirst, 1991) word relationship types. However, their greedy algorithm does not use a part-of-speech tagger. Instead, the algorithm only selects those words that contain noun entries in WordNet to compute Lexical Chains. But, as Barzilay and Elhadad (1997) point at, the use of a part-of-speech tagger could eliminate wrong inclusions of words such as *read*, which has both noun and verb entries in WordNet.

So, Barzilay and Elhadad (1997) propose the first dynamic method to compute Lexical Chains. They argue that the most appropriate sense of a word can only be chosen after examining all possible Lexical Chain combinations that can be generated from a text. Because all possible senses of the word are not taken into account, except at the time of insertion, potentially pertinent context information that is likely to appear after the word is lost. However, this method of retaining all possible interpretations until the end of the process, causes the exponential growth of the time and space complexity.

As a consequence, Silber and McCoy (2002) propose a linear time version of (Barzilay and Elhadad, 1997) lexical chaining algorithm. In particular, (Silber and McCoy, 2002)'s implementation creates a structure, called meta-chains, that implicitly stores

Proceedings of the Workshop on Information Extraction Beyond The Document, pages 36–47,
Sydney, July 2006. ©2006 Association for Computational Linguistics

all chain interpretations without actually creating them, thus keeping both the space and time usage of the program linear.

Finally, Galley and McKeown (2003) propose a chaining method that disambiguates nouns prior to the processing of Lexical Chains. Their evaluation shows that their algorithm is more accurate than (Barzilay and Elhadad, 1997) and (Silber and McCoy, 2002) ones.

One common point of all these works is that Lexical Chains are built using WordNet as the standard linguistic resource. Unfortunately, systems based on static linguistic knowledge bases are limited. First, such resources are difficult to find. Second, they are largely obsolete by the time they are available. Third, linguistic resources capture a particular form of lexical knowledge which is often very different from the sort needed to specifically relate words or sentences. In particular, WordNet is missing a lot of explicit links between intuitively related words. Fellbaum (1998) refers to such obvious omissions in WordNet as the "tennis problem" where nouns such as *nets*, *rackets* and *umpires* are all present, but WordNet provides no links between these related tennis concepts.

In order to solve these problems, we propose to automatically construct from a collection of documents a lexico-semantic knowledge base with the purpose to identify cohesive lexical relationships between words based on corpus evidence. This hierarchical lexico-semantic knowledge base is built by using the Pole-Based Overlapping Clustering Algorithm (Cleuziou et al., 2004) that clusters words with similar meanings and allows words with multiple meanings to belong to different clusters. The second step of the process aims at automatically extracting Lexical Chains from texts based on our knowledge base. For that purpose, we propose a new greedy algorithm which can be seen as an extension of (Hirst and St-Onge, 1997) and (Barzilay and Elhadad, 1997) algorithms which allows polysemous words to belong to different chains thus breaking the "one-word/one-concept per document" paradigm (Gale et al., 1992)[1]. In particular, it implements (Lin, 1998) information-theoretic definition of similarity as the relatedness criterion for the attribution of words to Lexical Chains[2].

2 Building a Similarity Matrix

In order to build the lexico-semantic knowledge base, the Pole-Based Overlapping Clustering Algorithm needs as input a similarity matrix that gathers the similarities between all the words in the corpus. For that purpose, we propose a contextual analysis of each nominal unit (nouns and compound nouns) in the corpus. In particular, each nominal unit is associated to a word context vector and the similarity between nominal units is calculated by the informative similarity measure proposed by (Dias and Alves, 2005).

2.1 Data Preparation

The context corpus is first pre-processed in order to extract nominal units from it. The TnT tagger (Brants, 2000) is first applied to our context corpus to morpho-syntactically mark all the words in it. Once all words have been morpho-syntactically tagged, we apply the statistically-based multiword unit extractor SENTA (Dias et al., 1999) that extracts multiword units based on any input text[3]. For example, multiword units are compound nouns (*free kick*), compound determinants (*an amount of*), verbal locutions (*to put forward*), adjectival locutions (*dark blue*) or institutionalized phrases (*con carne*). Finally, we use a set of well-known heuristics (Daille, 1995) to retrieve compound nouns using the idea that groups of words that correspond to a priori defined syntactical patterns such as *Adj+Noun, Noun+Noun, Noun+Prep+Noun* can be identified as compound nouns. Indeed, nouns usually convey most of the information in a written text. They are the main contributors to the "aboutness" of a text. For example, *free kick, city hall, operating system* are compound nouns which sense is not compositional i.e. the sense of the multiword unit can

[1]This characteristic can be interesting for multi-topic documents like web news stories. Indeed, in this case, there may be different topics in the same document as different news stories may appear. In some way, it follows the idea of (Krovetz, 1998).

[2]Of course, other similarity measures (Resnik, 1995; Jiang and Conrath, 1997; Leacock and Chodorow, 1998) could be implemented and should be evaluated in further work. However, we used (Lin, 1998) similarity measure as it has shown improved results for Lexical Chains construction.

[3]By choosing both the TnT tagger and the multiword unit extractor SENTA, we guarantee that our architecture remains as language-independent as possible.

not be expressed by the sum of its constituents senses. So, identifying lexico-semantic connections between nouns is an adequate means of determining cohesive ties between textual units[4].

2.2 Word Context Vectors

The similarity matrix is a matrix where each cell corresponds to a similarity value between two nominal units[5]. In this paper, we propose a contextual analysis of nominal units based on similarity between word context vectors.

Word context vectors are an automated method for representing information based on the local context of words in texts. So, for each nominal unit in the corpus, we associate an N-dimension vector consisting of its N most related words[6].

In order to find the most relevant co-occurrent nominal units, we implement the Symmetric Conditional Probability (Silva et al., 1999) which is defined in Equation 1 where $p(w_1, w_2)$, $p(w_1)$ and $p(w_2)$ are respectively the probability of co-occurrence of the nominal units w_1 and w_2 and the marginal probabilities of w_1 and w_2.

$$SCP(w_1, w_2) = \frac{p(w_1, w_2)^2}{p(w_1) \times p(w_2)} \quad (1)$$

In particular, the window context for the calculation of co-occurrence probabilities is settled to F=20 words. In fact, we count, in all the texts of the corpus, the number of occurrences of w_1 and w_2 appearing together in a window context of $F - 2$ words. So, $p(w_1, w_2)$ represents the density function computed as follows: the number of times w_1 and w_2 co-occur divided by the number of words in the corpus[7]. In the present work, the values of the $SCP(.,.)$ are not used as a factor of importance between words in the word context vector i.e. no differentiation is made in terms of relevance between the words within the word context vector. This issue will be tackled in future work[8].

[4]However, we acknowledge that verbs and adjectives should also be tackled in future work.

[5]Many works have been proposed on word similarity (Lin, 1998).

[6]In our experiments, N=10.

[7]We note that multiword units are counted as single words as when they are identified (e.g. President of the United States), they are re-written in the corpus by linking all single words with an underscore (e.g. President_of_the_United_States)

[8]We may point at the fact that satisfying results were obtained by the Symmetric Conditional Probability measure compared to the Pointwise Mutual Information for instance (Cleuziou et al., 2003)

2.3 Similarity between Context Vectors

The closeness of vectors in the space is equivalent to the closeness of the subject content. Thus, nominal units that are used in a similar local context will have vectors that are relatively close to each other. However, in order to define similarities between vectors, we must transform each word context vector into a high dimensional vector consisting of real-valued components. As a consequence, each co-occurring word of the word context vector is associated to a weight which evaluates its importance in the corpus.

2.3.1 Weighting score

The weighting score of any word in a document can be directly derived from an adaptation of the score proposed in (Dias and Alves, 2005). In particular, we consider the combination of two main heuristics: the well-known *tf.idf* measure proposed by (Salton et al., 1975) and a new density measure (Dias and Alves, 2005).

tf.idf: Given a word w and a document d, the $tf.idf(w,d)$ is defined in Equation 2 where $tf(w,d)$ is the number of occurrences of w in d, $|d|$ corresponds to the number of words in d, N is the number of documents in the corpus and $df(w)$ stands for the number of documents in the corpus in which the word w occurs.

$$tf.idf(w,d) = \frac{tf(w,d)}{|d|} \times \log_2\left(\frac{N}{df(w)}\right) \quad (2)$$

density: The basic idea of the word density measure is to evaluate the dispersion of a word within a document. So, very disperse words will not be as relevant as dense words. This density measure $dens(.,.)$ is defined in Equation 3.

$$dens(w,d) = \sum_{k=1}^{tf(w,d)-1} \frac{1}{\ln(dist(o_{(w,k)}, o_{(w,k+1)}) + e)} \quad (3)$$

For any given word w, its density $dens(w,d)$ is calculated from all the distances between all its occurrences in document d, $tf(w,d)$. So, $dist(o_{(w,k)}, o_{(w,k+1)})$ calculates the distance that separates two consecutive occurrences of w in terms of words within the document. In particular, e is the base of the natural logarithm so that $ln(e) = 1$. This argument is included into Equation 3 as it will give a density value of 1 for any word that only occurs once in the document. In fact, we give this word a high density value.

final weight: The weighting score $weight(w)$ of any word w in the corpus can be directly derived from the previous two heuristics. This score is defined in Equation 4 where $\overline{tf}$ and $\overline{dens}$ are respectively the average of $tf(.,.)$ and $dens(.,.)$ over all the documents in which the word w occurs i.e. N_w.

$$weight(w) = \overline{tf}.idf(w) \times \overline{dens}(w) \quad (4)$$

where $\overline{tf} = \frac{\sum_d tf(w,d)}{N_w}$ and $\overline{dens}(w) = \frac{\sum_d dens(w,d)}{N_w}$

2.3.2 Informative Similarity Measure

The next step aims at determining the similarity between all nominal units. Theoretically, a similarity measure can be defined as follows. Suppose that $X_i = (X_{i1}, X_{i2}, X_{i3}, , X_{ip})$ is a row vector of observations on p variables associated with a label i. The similarity between two words i and j is defined as $S_{ij} = f(X_i, X_j)$ where f is some function of the observed values. In the context of our work, X_i and X_j are 10-dimension word context vectors.

In order to avoid the lexical repetition problem of similarity measures, (Dias and Alves, 2005) have proposed an informative similarity measure called $infoSimBA$, which basic idea is to integrate into the Cosine measure, the word co-occurrence factor inferred from a collection of documents with the Symmetric Conditional Probability (Silva et al., 1999). See Equation 5.

$$InfoSimBA(X_i, X_j) = \frac{A_{ij}}{B_i \times B_j + A_{ij}} \quad (5)$$

where

$$A_{ij} = \sum_{k=1}^{p}\sum_{l=1}^{p} X_{ik} \times X_{jl} \times SCP(w_{ik}, w_{jl})$$

$$\forall i, B_i = \sqrt{\sum_{k=1}^{p}\sum_{l=1}^{p} X_{ik} \times X_{il} \times \text{SCP}(w_{ik}, w_{il})}$$

and any X_{zv} corresponds to the word weighting factor $weight(w_{zv})$, $SCP(w_{ik}, w_{jl})$ is the Symmetric Conditional Probability value between w_{ik}, the word that indexes the word context vector i at position k and w_{jl}, the word that indexes the word context vector j at position l.

In particular, this similarity measure has proved to lead to better results compared to the classical similarity measure (Cosine) and shares the same idea as the Latent Semantic Analysis (LSA) but in a different manner. Let's consider the following two sentences.

```
(1) Ronaldo defeated the goalkeeper once more.
```

```
(2) Real_Madrid_striker scored again.
```

It is clear that both sentences (1) and (2) are similar although they do not share any word in common. Such a situation would result in a null Cosine value so evidencing no relationship between (1) and (2). To solve this problem, the $InfoSimBA(.,.)$ function would calculate for each word in sentence (2), the product of its weight with each weight of all the words in sentence (1), and would then multiply this product by the degree of cohesiveness existing between those two words calculated by the Symmetric Conditional Probability measure. For example, *Real_Madrid_striker* would give rise to the sum of 6 products i.e. *Real_Madrid_striker* with *Ronaldo*, *Real_Madrid_striker* with *defeated* and so on and so forth. As a consequence, sentence (1) and (2) would show a high similarity as *Real_Madrid_striker* is highly related to *Ronaldo*.

Once the similarity matrix is built based on the $infoSimBA$ between all word context vectors of all nominal units in the corpus, we give it as input to the Pole-Based Overlapping Clustering Algorithm (Cleuziou et al., 2004) to build a hierarchy of concepts i.e. our lexico-semantic knowledge base.

3 Hierarchy of Concepts

Clustering is the task that structures units in such a way it reflects the semantic relations existing between them. In our framework nominal units are first grouped into overlapping clusters (or soft-clusters) such that final clusters correspond to conceptual classes (called "concepts" in the following). Then, concepts are hierarchically structured in order to capture semantic links between them.

Many clustering methods have been proposed in the data analysis research fields. Few of them propose overlapping clusters as output, in spite of the interest it represents for domains of application such as Natural Language Processing or Bioinformatics. PoBOC (*Pole-Based Overlapping Clustering*) (Cleuziou et al., 2004) and CBC (*Clustering By Committees*) (Pantel and Lin, 2002) are two clustering algorithms suitable for the word clustering task. They both proceed by first constructing tight clusters[9] and then assigning residual objects to their most similar tight clusters.

A recent comparative study (Cicurel et al., 2006) shows that CBC and PoBOC both lead to relevant results for the task of word clustering. Nevertheless CBC requires parameters hard to tune whereas PoBOC is free of any parametrization. The last argument encouraged us to use the PoBOC algorithm.

Unlike most of commonly used clustering algorithms, the Pole-Based Overlapping Clustering Algorithm shows the following advantages among others : (1) it requires no parameters i.e. input is restricted to a single similarity matrix, (2) the number of final clusters is automatically found and (3) it provides overlapping clusters allowing to take into account the different possible meanings of lexical units.

3.1 A Graph-based Approach

The Pole-Based Overlapping Clustering Algorithm is based on a graph-theoretical framework. Graph formalism is often used in the context of clustering (graph-clustering). It first consists in defining a graph structure which illustrates the data (vertices) with links (edges) between them and then in proposing a graph-partitioning process.

Numerous graph structures have been proposed (Estivill-Castro et al., 2001). They all consider the data set as set of vertices but differ on the way to decide that two vertices are connected. Some methodologies are listed below where V is the set of vertices, E the set of edges, $G(V, E)$ a graph and d a distance measure:

- Nearest Neighbor Graph (NNG) : each vertex is connected to its nearest neighbor,
- Minimum Spanning Tree (MST) : $\forall(x_i, x_j) \in V \times V$ a path exists between x_i and x_j in G with $\sum_{(x_i,x_j)\in E} d(x_i, x_j)$ minimized,
- Relative Neighborhood Graph (RNG) : x_i and x_j are connected iff $\forall x_k \in V \setminus \{x_i, x_j\}$, $d(x_i, x_j) \leq \max\{d(x_i, x_k), d(x_j, x_k)\}$
- Gabriel Graph (GG) : x_i and x_j are connected iff the circle with diameter $\overline{x_i x_j}$ is empty,
- Delaunay Triangulation (DT) : x_i and x_j are connected iff the associated Voronoi cells are adjacent.

In particular, an inclusion order exists on these graphs. One can show that $NNG \subseteq MST \subseteq RNG \subseteq GG \subseteq DT$.

The choice of the suitable graph structure depends on the expressiveness we want an edge to capture and the partitioning process we plan to perform. The Pole-Based Overlapping Clustering Algorithm aims at retrieving dense subsets in *a graph where two similar data are connected and two dissimilar ones are disconnected.* Noticing that previous structures do not match with this definition of a proximity-graph[10], a new variant is proposed with the Pole-Based Overlapping Clustering Algorithm in definition 3.1.

Definition 3.1 *Given a similarity measure s on a data set X, the graph (denoted $G_s(V, E)$) is defined by the set of vertices $V = X$ and the set of edges E such that* $(x_i, x_j) \in E \Leftrightarrow x_i \in \mathcal{N}(x_j) \wedge x_j \in \mathcal{N}(x_i)$.

In particular, $\mathcal{N}(x_i)$ corresponds to the local neighborhood of x_i built as in equation 6.

$$\mathcal{N}(x_i) = \{x_j \in X | s(x_i, x_j) > s(x_i, X)\} \quad (6)$$

where the notation $s(x_i, I)$ denotes the average similarity of x_i with the set of objects I i.e.

$$\sum_{x_k \in I} \frac{s(x_i, x_k)}{|I|} \quad (7)$$

This definition of neighborhood is a way to avoid requiring to a parameter that would be too dependent of the similarity used. Furthermore, the use of local neighborhoods avoids the use of arbitrary thresholds which mask the variations of densities. Indeed, clusters are extracted from a similarity graph which differs from traditional proximity graphs (Jaromczyk and Toussaint, 1992) in the definition of local

[9]The tight clusters are called "committees" in CBC and "poles" in PoBOC.

[10]Indeed, for instance, all of these graphs connect an outlier with at least one other vertex. This is not the case with PoBOC.

neighborhoods which condition edges in the graph. Neighborhood is different for each object and is computed on the basis of similarities with all other objects. Finally, an edge connects two vertices if they are both contained in the neighborhood of the other one. Figure 1 illustrates the neighborhood constraint above. In this case, as x_i and x_j are not both in the intersection, they would not be connected.

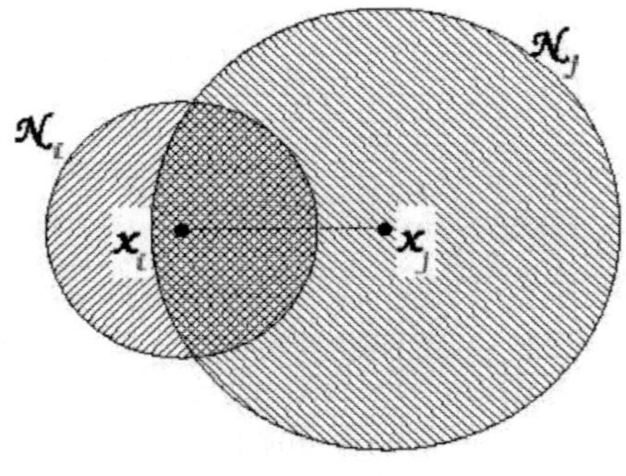

Figure 1: To be connected, both x_i and x_j must be in the intersection.

3.2 Discovery of Poles

The graph representation helps to discover a set of fully-connected subgraphs (cliques) highly separated, denoted as Poles. Because $G_s(V, E)$ is built such that two vertices x_i and x_j are connected if and only if they are similar[11], a clique has the required properties to be a good cluster. Indeed, such a cluster guarantees that all its constituents are similar.

The search of maximal cliques in a graph is an NP-complete problem. As a consequence, heuristics are used in order to (1) build a great clique around a starting vertex (Bomze et al., 1999) and (2) choose the starting vertices in such a way cliques are as distant as possible.

Given a starting vertex x, the first heuristic consists in adding iteratively the vertex x_i which satisfies the following conditions:

- x_i is connected to each vertex in P (with P the clique/Pole in construction),
- among the connected vertices, x_i is the nearest one in average ($s(x_i, P)$).

[11] In the sense that x_i (resp. x_j) is more similar to x_j (resp. x_i) than to other data on average.

As a consequence, initialized with $P = \{x\}$, the clique then grows until no vertex can be added.

The second heuristic guides the selection of the starting vertices in a simple manner. Given a set of Poles $P_1, \ldots, P_m$ already extracted, we select the vertex x as in Equation 8.

$$s(x, P_1 \cup \cdots \cup P_m) = \min_{x_i} s(x_i, P_1 \cup \cdots \cup P_m) \quad (8)$$

A new Pole is then built from x if and only if x satisfies the following conditions:

- $\forall k \in \{1, \ldots, m\},\ x \notin P_k$,
- $s(x, P_1 \cup \cdots \cup P_m) < s(X, X) = \frac{1}{|X|^2} \sum_{x_i} \sum_{x_j} s(x_i, x_j)$

Poles are thus extracted while $P_1 \cup \cdots \cup P_m \neq X$ and the next starting vertex x is far enough from the previous Poles. In particular, as Poles represent the seeds of the further final clusters, this heuristic gives no restriction on the number of clusters. The first Pole is obtained from the starting point x^* that checks Equation 9.

$$x^* = \arg\min_{x_k \in X} s(x_k, X) \quad (9)$$

3.3 Multi-Assignment

Once the Poles are built, the Pole-Based Overlapping Clustering algorithm uses them as clusters representatives. Membership functions $m(.,.)$ are defined in order to assign each object to its nearest Poles as shown in Equation 10.

$$\forall x_i \in X,\ P_j \in \{P_1, \ldots, P_m\} : m(x_i, P_j) = s(x_i, P_j) \quad (10)$$

For each object x_i to assign, the set of poles is ordered $(P_1(x_i), \ldots, P_m(x_i))$ such that $P_1(x_i)$ denotes the nearest pole[12] for x_i, $P_2(x_i)$ the second nearest pole for x_i and so on. We first assign x_i to its closest Pole ($P_1(x_i)$). Then, for each pole $P_k(x_i)$(in the order previously defined) we decide to assign x_i to $P_k(x_i)$ if it satisfies to the following two conditions :

- $\forall k' < k$, x_i is assigned to $P_{k'}(x_i)$,
- if $k < m$,

$$s(x_i, P_k(x_i)) \geq \frac{s(x_i, P_{k-1}(x_i)) + s(x_i, P_{k+1}(x_i))}{2}$$

This methodology results into a coverage of the starting data set with overlapping clusters (extended Poles).

[12] $P_1(x_i) = \arg\max_{P_j} s(x_i, P_j)$

3.4 Hierarchical Organization

A final step consists in organizing the obtained clusters into a hierarchical tree. This structure is useful to catch the topology of a set of a priori disconnected groups. The Pole-Based Overlapping Clustering algorithm integrates this stage and proceeds by successive merging of the two nearest clusters like for usual agglomerative approaches (Sneath and Sokal, 1973). In this process, the similarity between two clusters is obtained by the average-link (or complete-link) method:

$$s(I_p, I_q) = \frac{1}{|I_p|.|I_q|} \sum_{x_i \in I_p} \sum_{x_j \in I_q} s(x_i, x_j) \quad (11)$$

To deal with overlapping clusters we considere in Equation 11 the similarity between an object and itself to be equal to 1 : $s(x_i, x_i) = 1$.

4 Lexical Chaining Algorithm

Once the lexico-semantic knowledge base has been built, it is possible to use it for Lexical Chaining. In this section, we propose a new greedy algorithm which can be seen as an extension of (Hirst and St-Onge, 1997) and (Barzilay and Elhadad, 1997) algorithms as it allows polysemous words to belong to different chains thus breaking the "one-word/one-concept per document" paradigm (Gale et al., 1992). Indeed, multi-topic documents like web news stories may introduce different topics in the same document/url and do not respect the "one sense per discourse" paradigm. As we want to deal with real-world applications, this characteristic may show interesting results for the specific task of Text Summarization for Web documents. Indeed, comparatively to the experiments made by (Gale et al., 1992) that deal with "well written discourse", web documents show unusual discourse structures. In some way, our algorithm follows the idea of (Krovetz, 1998). Finally, it implements (Lin, 1998)'s information-theoretic definition of similarity as the relatedness criterion for the attribution of words to Lexical Chains.

4.1 Algorithm

Our chaining algorithm is based on both approaches of (Barzilay and Elhadad, 1997) and (Hirst and St-Onge, 1997). So, our chaining model is developed according to all possible alternatives of word senses. In fact, all senses of a word are defined by the clusters the word appears in[13]. We present our algorithm below.

```
Begin with no chain.
 For all distinct nominal units in text order do
  For all its senses do
    a) - among present chains find the sense
         which satisfies the relatedness
         criterion and link the new word to
         this chain.
       - Remove unappropriate senses of the
         new word and the chain members.
    b)if no sense is close enough, start a new chain.
  End For
 End For
End
```

4.2 Assignment of a word to a Lexical Chain

In order to assign a word to a given Lexical Chain, we need to evaluate the degree of relatedness of the given word to the words in the chain. This is done by evaluating the relatedness between all the clusters present in the Lexical Chain and all the clusters in which the word appears.

4.2.1 Scoring Function

In order to determine if two clusters are semantically related, we use our lexico-semantic knowledge base and apply (Lin, 1998)'s measure of semantic similarity defined in Equation 12.

$$simLin(C_1, C_2) = \frac{2 \times \log P(C_0)}{\log P(C_1) + \log P(C_2)} \quad (12)$$

The computation of Equation 12 is illustrated below using the fragment of WordNet in Figure 2.

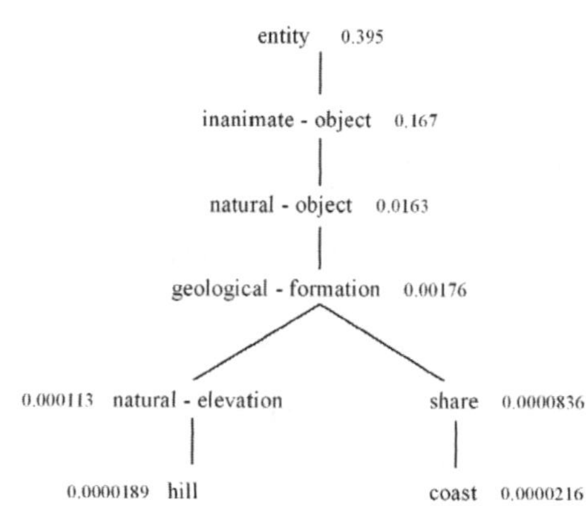

Figure 2: Fragment of WordNet (Lin, 1998).

[13]From now on, for presentation purposes, we will take as synonymous the words *clusters* and *senses*

In this case, it would be easy to compute the similarity between the concepts of *hill* and *coast* where the number attached to each node C is $P(C)$. It is shown in Equation 13.

$$simLin(hill, coast) = \frac{2 \log P(geological - formation)}{\log P(hill) + \log P(coast)} = 0.59 \quad (13)$$

However, in our taxonomy, as in any knowledge base computed by hierarchical clustering algorithms, only leaves contain words. So, upper clusters (i.e. nodes) in the taxonomy gather all distinct words that appear in the clusters they subsume. We present this situation in Figure 3.

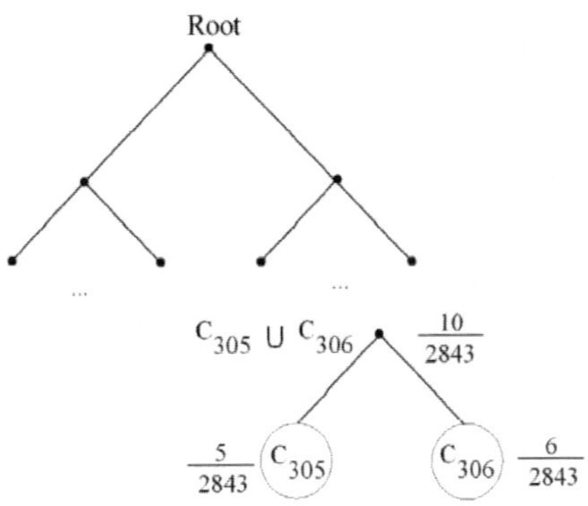

Figure 3: Fragment of our taxonomy.

In particular, clusters C_{305} and C_{306} of our hierarchical tree, for the domain of Economy, are represented by the following sets of words C_{305} ={life, effort, stability, steps, negotiations} and C_{306} ={steps, restructure, corporations, abuse, interests, ministers} and the number attached to each node C is $P(C)$ calculated as in Equation 14[14].

$$P(C_i) = \frac{\text{\# of words in the cluster}}{\text{\# of distinct words in all clusters}} \quad (14)$$

4.2.2 Relatedness criterion

The relatedness criterion is the threshold that needs to be respected in order to assign a word to a Lexical Chain. In fact, it works like a threshold. In this case, it is based on the average semantic similarity between all the clusters present in the taxonomy. So, if all semantic similarities between a candidate word cluster C_k and all the clusters in the chain $\forall l, C_l$ respect the relatedness criterion, the word is assigned to the Lexical Chain. This situation is defined in Equation 15 where c is a constant to be tuned and n is the number of words in the taxonomy. So, if Equation 15 is satisfied, the word w with cluster C_k is agglomerated to the Lexical Chain.

$$\forall l, simLin(C_k, C_l) > c \times \frac{\sum_{i=0}^{n} \sum_{j=i+1}^{n} simLin(C_i, C_j)}{\frac{n^2}{2} - n} \quad (15)$$

In the following section, we present an example of our algorithm.

4.2.3 Example of the Lexical Chain algorithm

The example below illustrates our Lexical Chain algorithm. Let's consider that a node is created for the first nominal unit encountered in the text i.e. *crisis* with its sense (C_{31}). The next appearing candidate word is *recession* which has two senses (C_{29} and C_{34}). Considering a relatedness criterion equal to 0.81 and the following similarities, $simLin(C_{31}, C_{29}) = 0.87$, $simLin(C_{31}, C_{34}) = 0.82$, the choice of the sense for *recession* splits the Lexical Chain into two different interpretations as shown in Figure 4, as both similarities overtake the given threshold 0.81.

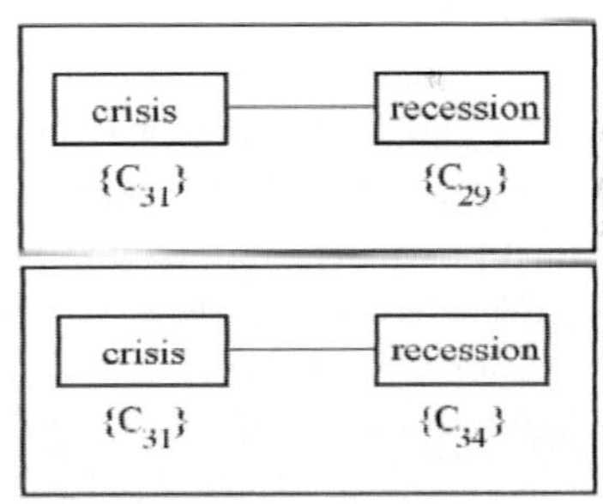

Figure 4: Interpretations 1 and 2.

The next candidate word *trouble* has also two senses (C_{29} and C_{32}). As all the words in a Lexical Chain influence each other in the selection of the respective senses of the new word considered, we have the following situation in Figure 5.

So, three cases can happen: (1) all similarities overtake the threshold and we must consider both representations, (2) only the similarities related to one representation overtake the threshold and we

[14]The value 2843 in Figure 3 is the total number of distinct words in our concept hierarchy.

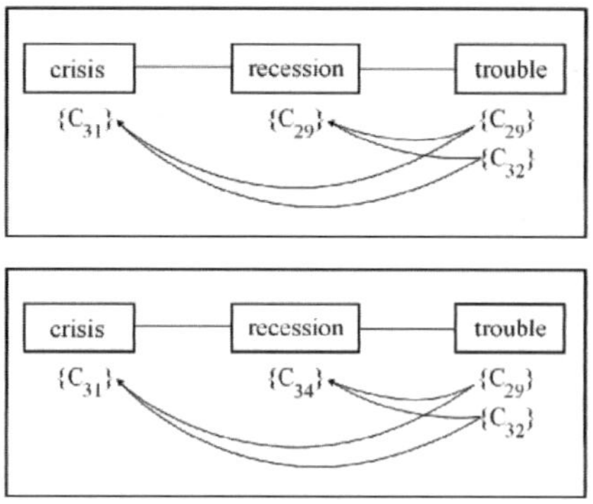

Figure 5: Selection of senses.

only consider this representation or (3) none of the similarities overtake the threshold and we create a new Lexical Chain. So, we proceed with our algorithm for both interpretations.

Interpretation 1 shows the following similarities $simLin(C_{31}, C_{29}) = 0.87$, $simLin(C_{31}, C_{32}) = 0.75$, $simLin(C_{29}, C_{29}) = 1.0$, $simLin(C_{29}, C_{32}) = 0.78$ and interpretation 2 the following ones, $simLin(C_{31}, C_{29}) = 0.87$, $simLin(C_{31}, C_{32}) = 0.75$, $simLin(C_{34}, C_{29}) = 0.54$, $simLin(C_{34}, C_{32}) = 0.55$.

By computing the average similarities for interpretations 1 and 2, we reach the following results: $average(Interpretation1) = 0.85 > 0.81$ and $average(Interpretation2) = 0.68 \not> 0.81$.

As a consequence, the word *trouble* is inserted in the Lexical Chain with the appropriate sense (C_{29}) as it maximizes the overall similarity of the chain and the chain members senses are updated. In this example, the interpretation with (C_{32}) is discarded as is the cluster (C_{34}) for *recession*. This processing is described in Figure 6.

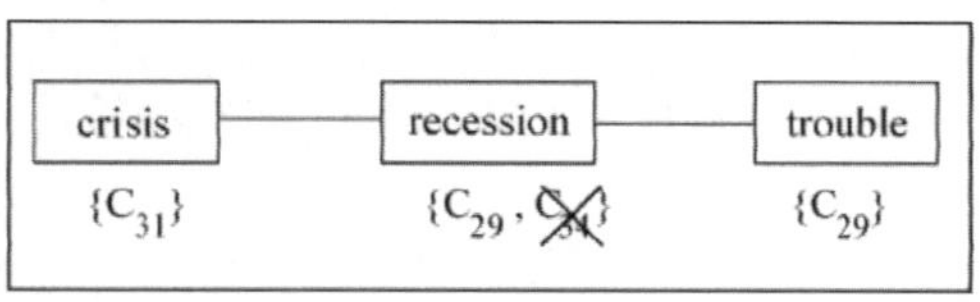

Figure 6: Selection of appropriate senses.

4.2.4 Score of a chain

Once all chains have been computed, only the high-scoring ones must be picked up as representing the important concepts of the original document. Therefore, one must first identify the strongest chains. Like in (Barzilay and Elhadad, 1997), we define a chain score which is defined in Equation 16 where $|chain|$ is the number of words in the chain.

$$score(chain) = \frac{\sum_{i=0}^{|chain|-1} \sum_{j=i+1}^{|chain|} simLin(C_i, C_j)}{\frac{(|chain| - 1)|chain|}{2}} \quad (16)$$

As all chains will be scored, the ones with higher scores will be extracted. Of course, a threshold will have to be defined by the user. In the next section, we will show some qualitative and quantitative results of our architecture.

5 Evaluation

The evaluation of Lexical Chains is generally difficult. Even if they can be effectively used in many practical applications, Lexical Chains are seldom desirable outputs in a real-world application, and it is unclear how to assess their quality independently of the underlying application in which they are used (Budanitsky and Hirst, 2006). For example, in Summarization, it is hard to determine whether a good or bad performance comes from the efficiency of the lexical chaining algorithm or from the appropriateness of using Lexical Chains in that kind of application. It is also true that some work has been done in this direction (Budanitsky and Hirst, 2006) by collecting Human Lexical Chains to compare against automatically built Lexical Chains. However, this type of evaluation is logistically impossible to perform as we aim at developing a system that does not depend on any language or topic. So, in this section, we will only present some results generated by our architecture (like (Barzilay and Elhadad, 1997; Teich and Fankhauser, 2004) do), although we acknowledge that other comparative evaluations (with WordNet, with Human Lexical Chains or within independent applications like Text Summarization) must be done in order to draw definitive conclusions.

We have generated four taxonomies from four different domains (Sport, Economy, Politics and War) from a set of documents of the DUC 2004[15]. Moreover, we have extracted Lexical Chains for all four

[15] http://duc.nist.gov/duc2004/

domains to show the ability of our system to switch from domain to domain without any problem.

5.1 Quantitative Function

Four texts from each domain of the DUC 2004 corpus have been used to extract Lexical Chains based on the four knowledge bases built from all texts of DUC 2004 for each one of the four following domains: Sport, Economy, Politics and War. However, in this section, we will only present the results from the Sport Domain as results show similar behaviors for the other domains. In particular, we present in Table 1 the characteristics of each document.

	# Words	#Distinct Words	#Distinct Nouns
Doc 1	8133	1956	672
Doc 2	3823	1630	708
Doc 3	4594	953	324
Doc 4	4530	1265	431

Table 1: Characteristics of Documents for Sport

The first interesting conclusion shown in Table 2 is that the number of Lexical Chains does not depend on the document size but rather on the nominal units distribution. Indeed, for example, the number of words in Document 1 is twice as big as in Document 2. Although, we have more Lexical Chains in Document 2 than in Document 1, as Document 2 has more distinct nominal units.

	c=5	c=6	c=7	c=8
Doc 1	27	43	73	73
Doc 2	31	52	81	83
Doc 3	28	40	51	51
Doc 4	29	53	83	87

Table 2: # Lexical Chains per Document

The second interesting conclusion is that our algorithm does not gather words that belong to only one cluster and take advantage of the automatically built lexico-semantic knowledge base. This is illustrated in Table 3. However, it is obvious that by increasing the constant c the words in a chain tend to belong to only one cluster as it is the case for most of the best Lexical Chains with $c = 8$.

5.2 Qualitative Evaluation

In this section, as it is done in (Barzilay and Elhadad, 1997; Teich and Fankhauser, 2004), we present the five highest-scoring chains for the best threshold that we experimentally evaluated to be $c = 7$ for each domain (See Tables 4, 5, 6, 7). It is clear that the obtained Lexical Chains show a desirable degree of representativeness of the text in analysis.

	c=5	c=6	c=7	c=8
Doc 1	19	13	7	7
Doc 2	13	6	3	3
Doc 3	3	4	4	4
Doc 4	6	4	3	3

Table 3: # Clusters per Lexical Chain

Domain=Sport, Document=3, c=7
- #0, 1 cluster and score=1.0: {United States, couple, competition}
- #6, 3 clusters and score=1.0: {boats, Sunday night, sailor, Sword, Orion, veteran, cutter, Winston Churchill, Solo Globe, Challenger, navy, Race, supposition, instructions, responsibility, skipper, east, Melbourne, deck, kilometer, masts, bodies, races, GMT, Admiral's, Cups, Britain, Star, Class, Atlanta, Seattle, arms, fatality, sea, waves, dark, yacht's, Dad, Guy's, son, Mark, beer, talk, life, Richard, Winning, affair, canopy, death}
- #9, 1 cluster and score=1.0: {record, days, hours, minutes, rescue}
- #16, 3 clusters and score=1.0: {Snow, shape, north, easters, thunder, storm, change, knots, west, level, maxi's, search, Authority, seas, helicopter, night vision, equipment, feet, rescues, Campbell, suffering, hypothermia, safety, foot, sailors, colleagues, Hospital, deaths, bodies, fatality}
- #19, 2 clusters and score=1.0: {challenge, crew, Monday, VC, Offshore, Stand, Newcastle, mid morning, Eden, Rescuers, aircraft, unsure, whereabouts, killing, contact}

Table 4: 5 best Lexical Chains for Sport

Domain=Economy, Document=5, c=7
- #88, 4 clusters and score=1.0: {sign, chance, Rio, Janeiro, Grande, Sul, uphill, promise, hospitals, powerhouse, success, inhabitants, victory, pad, presidency, contingent, exit, legislature}
- #50, 1 cluster and score=1.0: {transactions, taxes, Stabilization, spate, fuel, income, fortunes, means}
- #77, 1 cluster and score=1.0: {proposal, factory, owners, Fund, Rubin's}
- #126, 1 cluster and score=1.0: {disaster, control, investment, review}
- #12, 2 clusters and score=0.99: {issue, order, University, population, question, timing, currencies}

Table 5: 5 best Lexical Chains for Economy

For instance, the Lexical Chain #16 in the domain of Sport clearly exemplifies the tragedy of climbers that were killed in a sudden change of weather in the mountains and who could not be rescued by the authorities.

However, some Lexical Chains are less expressive. For instance, it is not clear what the Lexical Chain #40 expresses in the domain of Politics. Indeed, none of the words present in the chain seem

Domain=Politics, Document=3, c=7
- #5, 1 cluster and score=1.0: {report, leaders, lives, information}
- #33, 1 cluster and score=1.0: {past, attention, defenders, investigations}
- #28, 2 clusters and score=0.95: {investigators, hospital, ward, wounds, neck, description, fashion, suspects, raids, assault, rifles, door, further details, surgery, service, detective, Igor, Kozhevnikov, Ministry}
- #40, 2 clusters and score=0.92: {security, times, weeks, fire}
- #24, 3 clusters and score=0.85: {enemies, Choice, stairwell, assailants, woman, attackers, entrance, car, guns, Friends, relatives, Mrs. Staravoitova, founder, movement, well thought, Sergei, Kozyrev, Association, Societies, supporter, Stalin's, council, criminals, Yegor, Gaidar, minister, ally, suggestions, measures, smile, commitment}

Table 6: 5 best Lexical Chains for Politics

Domain=War, Document=1, c=7
- #25, 2 clusters and score=1.0: {lightning, advance, Africa's, nation, outskirts, capital Kinshasa, troops, Angola, Zimbabwe, Namibia, chunk, routes, Katanga, Eastern, Kasai, provinces, copper}
- #53, 1 cluster and score=1.0: {Back, years, Ngeyo, farm, farmers, organization, breadbasket, quarter, century, businessman, hotels, tourist, memory, rivalry, rebellions}
- #56, 1 cluster and score=1.0: {political, freedoms, Hutus, Mai-Mai, warriors, Hunde, Nande, militiamen, Rwanda, ideology, weapons, persecution, landowners, ranchers, anarchy, Safari, Ngezayo, farmer, hotel, owner, camps}
- #24, 2 clusters and score=0.87: {fighting, people, leaders, diplomats, cause, president, Washington, U.S, units, weeks}
- #51, 2 clusters and score=0.82: {West, buildings, sight, point, tourists, mountain, gorillas, shops, guest, disputes}

Table 7: 5 best Lexical Chains for War

to express any idea about Politics. Moreover, due to the small number of inter-related nominal units within the Lexical Chain, this one can not be understood as it is without context. In fact, it was related to problems of car firing that have been occurring in the past few weeks and provoked security problems in the town.

Although some Lexical Chains are understandable as they are, most of them must be replaced in their context to fully understand their representativeness of the topics or subtopics of the text being analyzed. As a consequence, we deeply believe that Lexical Chains must be evaluated in the context of Natural Language Processing applications (such as Text Summarization (Doran et al., 2004)), as comparing Lexical Chains as they are is a very difficult task to tackle which may even lead to inconclusive results.

6 Conclusions and Future Work

In this paper, we implemented a greedy Language-Independent algorithm for building Lexical Chains. For that purpose, we first constructed a lexico-semantic knowledge base by applying the Pole-Based Overlapping Clustering algorithm (Cleuziou et al., 2004) to word-context vectors obtained by the application of the $SCP(.,.)$ measure (Silva et al., 1999) and the $InfoSimBA(.,.)$ (Dias and Alves, 2005) similarity measure. In a second step, we implemented (Lin, 1998)'s similarity measure and used it to define the relatedness criterion in order to assign a given word to a given chain in the lexical chaining process. Finally, our experimental evaluation shows that relevant Lexical Chains can be constructed with our lexical chaining algorithm, although we acknowledge that more comparative evaluations must be done in order to draw definitive conclusions. In particular, in future work, we want to compare our methodology using WordNet as the basic knowledge base, implement different similarity measures (Resnik, 1995; Jiang and Conrath, 1997; Leacock and Chodorow, 1998), experiment different Lexical Chains algorithms (Hirst and St-Onge, 1997; Barzilay and Elhadad, 1997; Galley and McKeown, 2003), scale our greedy algorithm for real-world applications following (Silber and McCoy, 2002) ideas and finally evaluate our system in independent Natural Language Processing applications such as Text Summarization (Doran et al., 2004).

References

R. Barzilay and M. Elhadad. 1997. *Using Lexical Chains for Text Summarization.* Proceedings of the Intelligent Scalable Text Summarization Workshop (ISTS-97), ACL, Madrid, Spain, pages 10-18.

I. Bomze, M. Budinich, P. Pardalos, and M. Pelillo. 1999. *The Maximum Clique Problem.* Handbook of Combinatorial Optimization, volume 4. Kluwer Academic publishers, Boston, MA.

T. Brants. 2000. *TnT - a Statistical Part-of-Speech Tagger.* In Proceedings of the 6th Applied NLP Conference, ANLP-2000. Seattle, WA.

A. Budanitsky and G. Hirst. 2006. *Evaluating WordNet-based Measures of Lexical Semantic Relatedness.* In Computational Linguistics, 32(1). pages: 13-47.

L. Cicurel, S. Bloehdorn and P. Cimiano. 2006. *Clustering of Polysemic Words.* In Advances in Data Analysis - 30th Annual Conference of the German Classification Society (GfKl). Berlin, Germany, March 8-10.

G. Cleuziou, L. Martin, and C. Vrain. 2004. *PoBOC: an Overlapping Clustering Algorithm. Application to Rule-Based Classication and Textual Data.* In Proceedings of the 16th European Conference on Artificial Intelligence, pages 440-444, Spain, August 22-27.

G. Cleuziou, V. Clavier, L. Martin. 2003. *Une Méthode de Regroupement de Mots Fondée sur la Recherche de Cliques dans un Graphe de Cooccurrences.* In Proceedings of Rencontres Terminologie et Intelligence Artificielle, France. pages 179-182.

B. Daille. 1995. *Study and Implementation of Combined Techniques for Automatic Extraction of Terminology.* In The balancing act combining symbolic and statistical approaches to language. MIT Press.

G. Dias and E. Alves. 2005. *Unsupervised Topic Segmentation Based on Word Co-occurrence and Multi-Word Units for Text Summarization.* In Proceedings of the ELECTRA Workshop associated to 28th ACM SIGIR Conference, Salvador, Brazil, pages 41-48.

G. Dias, S. Guilloré and J.G.P. Lopes. 1999. *Language Independent Automatic Acquisition of Rigid Multiword Units from Unrestricted Text Corpora.* In Proceedings of 6th Annual Conference on Natural Language Processing, Cargèse, France, pages 333-339.

W. Doran, N. Stokes, J. Carthy and J. Dunnion. 2004. *Assessing the Impact of Lexical Chain Scoring Methods and Sentence Extraction Schemes on Summarization.* In Proc. of the 5th Conference on Intelligent Text Processing and Computational Linguistics.

V. Estivill-Castro, I. Lee, and A. T. Murray. 2001. *Criteria on Proximity Graphs for Boundary Extraction and Spatial Clustering.* In Proceedings of the 5th Pacific-Asia Conference on Knowledge Discovery and Data Mining, Springer Verlag. pages 348-357.

C.D. Fellbaum. 1998. *WordNet: An Electronic Lexical Database.* MIT Press, New York.

W. Gale, K. Church, and D. Yarowsky. 1992. *One Sense per Discourse.* In Proceedings of the DARPA Speech and Natural Language Workshop.

M. Galley and K. McKeown. 2003. *Improving Word Sense Disambiguation in Lexical Chaining.* In Proceedings of 18th International Joint Conference on Artificial Intelligence (IJCAI'03), Acapulco, Mexico.

G. Hirst and D. St-Onge. 1997. *Lexical Chains as Representation of Context for the Detection and Correction of Malapropisms.* In WordNet: An electronic lexical database and some of its applications. MIT Press.

J.W. Jaromczyk and G.T. Toussaint. 1992. *Relative Neighborhood Graphs and Their Relatives.* P-IEEE, 80, pages 1502-1517.

J.J. Jiang and D.W. Conrath. 1997. *Semantic Similarity Based on Corpus Statistics and Lexical Taxonomy.* In Proceedings of International Conference on Research in Computational Linguistics, Taiwan.

R. Krovetz. 1998. *More than One Sense per Discourse.* NEC Princeton NJ Labs., Research Memorandum.

C. Leacock and M. Chodorow. 1998. *Combining Local Context and WordNet Similarity for Word Sense Identification.* In C. Fellbaum, editor, WordNet: An electronic lexical database. MIT Press. pages 265-283.

D. Lin. 1998. *An Information-theoretic Definition of Similarity.* In 15th International Conference on Machine Learning. Morgan Kaufmann, San Francisco.

G. Miller. 1995. *WordNet: An Lexical Database for English.* Communications of the Association for Computing Machinery (CACM), 38(11), pages 39-41.

J. Morris and G. Hirst. 1991. *Lexical Cohesion Computed by Thesaural Relations as an Indicator of the Structure of Text.* Computational Linguistics, 17(1).

P. Pantel and D. Lin. 2002. *Discovering Word Senses from Text.* In Proceedings of the Eighth ACM SIGKDD International Conference on Knowledge Discovery and Data Mining. pages 613-619.

P. Resnik. 1995. *Using Information Content to Evaluate Semantic Similarity.* In Proceedings of the 14th International Joint Conference on Artificial Intelligence, Montreal. pages 448-453.

P.M. Roget. 1852. *Roget's Thesaurus of English Words and Phrases.* Harlow, Essex, England: Longman.

G. Salton, C.S. Yang and C.T. Yu. 1975. *A Theory of Term Importance in Automatic Text Analysis.* In American Society of Information Science, 26(1).

G. Silber and K. McCoy. 2002. *Efficiently Computed Lexical Chains as an Intermediate Representation for Automatic Text Summarization.* Computational Linguistics, 28(4), pages 487-496.

J. Silva, G. Dias, S. Guilloré and J.G.P. Lopes. 1999. *Using LocalMaxs Algorithm for the Extraction of Contiguous and Non-contiguous Multiword Lexical Units.* In Proceedings of 9th Portuguese Conference in Artificial Intelligence. Springer-Verlag.

P. H. A. Sneath and R. R. Sokal. 1973. *Numerical Taxonomy - The Principles and Practice of Numerical Classification.* San Francisco, Freeman and Co.

E. Teich and P. Fankhauser. 2004. *Exploring Lexical Patterns in Text: Lexical Cohesion Analysis with WordNet.* In Proceedings of the 2nd International Wordnet Conference, Brno, Czech Republic. pages 326-331.

Data Selection in Semi-supervised Learning for Name Tagging

Heng Ji **Ralph Grishman**
Department of Computer Science
New York University
New York, NY, 10003, USA
hengji@cs.nyu.edu grishman@cs.nyu.edu

Abstract

We present two semi-supervised learning techniques to improve a state-of-the-art multi-lingual name tagger. For English and Chinese, the overall system obtains 1.7% - 2.1% improvement in F-measure, representing a 13.5% - 17.4% relative reduction in the spurious, missing, and incorrect tags. We also conclude that simply relying upon large corpora is not in itself sufficient: we must pay attention to unlabeled data selection too. We describe effective measures to automatically select documents and sentences.

1 Introduction

When applying machine learning approaches to natural language processing tasks, it is time-consuming and expensive to hand-label the large amounts of training data necessary for good performance. Unlabeled data can be collected in much larger quantities. Therefore, a natural question is whether we can use unlabeled data to build a more accurate learner, given the same amount of labeled data. This problem is often referred to as semi-supervised learning. It significantly reduces the effort needed to develop a training set. It has shown promise in improving the performance of many tasks such as name tagging (Miller et al., 2004), semantic class extraction (Lin et al., 2003), chunking (Ando and Zhang, 2005), coreference resolution (Bean and Riloff, 2004) and text classification (Blum and Mitchell, 1998).

However, it is not clear, when semi-supervised learning is applied to improve a learner, how the system should effectively select unlabeled data, and how the size and relevance of data impact the performance.

In this paper we apply two semi-supervised learning algorithms to improve a state-of-the-art name tagger. We run the baseline name tagger on a large unlabeled corpus (bootstrapping) and the test set (self-training), and automatically generate high-confidence machine-labeled sentences as additional 'training data'. We then iteratively retrain the model on the increased 'training data'.

We first investigated whether we can improve the system by simply using a lot of unlabeled data. By dramatically increasing the size of the corpus with unlabeled data, we did get a significant improvement compared to the baseline system. But we found that adding off-topic unlabeled data sometimes makes the performance worse. Then we tried to select relevant documents from the unlabeled data in advance, and got clear further improvements. We also obtained significant improvement by self-training (bootstrapping on the test data) without any additional unlabeled data.

Therefore, in contrast to the claim in (Banko and Brill, 2001), we concluded that, for some applications, effective use of large unlabeled corpora demands good data selection measures. We propose and quantify some effective measures to select documents and sentences in this paper.

The rest of this paper is structured as follows. Section 2 briefly describes the efforts made by previous researchers to use semi-supervised learning as well as the work of (Banko and Brill, 2001). Section 3 presents our baseline name tagger. Section 4 describes the motivation for our approach while Section 5 presents the details of two semi-supervised learning methods. Section 6 presents and discusses the experimental results on both English and Chinese. Section 7 presents our conclusions and directions for future work.

2 Prior Work

This work presented here extends a substantial body of previous work (Blum and Mitchell, 1998; Riloff and Jones, 1999; Ando and Zhang, 2005)

Proceedings of the Workshop on Information Extraction Beyond The Document, pages 48–55,
Sydney, July 2006.

that all focus on reducing annotation requirements. For the specific task of named entity annotation, some researchers have emphasized the creation of taggers from minimal seed sets (Strzalkowski and Wang, 1996; Collins and Singer, 1999; Lin et al., 2003) while another line of inquiry (which we are pursuing) has sought to improve on high-performance baseline taggers (Miller et al., 2004).

Banko and Brill (2001) suggested that the development of very large training corpora may be most effective for progress in empirical natural language processing. Their experiments show a logarithmic trend in performance as corpus size increases without performance reaching an upper bound. Recent work has replicated their work on thesaurus extraction (Curran and Moens, 2002) and is-a relation extraction (Ravichandran et al., 2004), showing that collecting data over a very large corpus significantly improves system performance. However, (Curran, 2002) and (Curran and Osborne, 2002) claimed that the choice of statistical model is more important than relying upon large corpora.

3 Motivation

The performance of name taggers has been limited in part by the amount of labeled training data available. How can an unlabeled corpus help to address this problem? Based on its original training (on the labeled corpus), there will be some tags (in the unlabeled corpus) that the tagger will be very sure about. For example, there will be contexts that were always followed by a person name (e.g., "*Capt.*") in the training corpus. If we find a new token *T* in this context in the unlabeled corpus, we can be quite certain it is a person name. If the tagger can learn this fact about *T*, it can successfully tag *T* when it appears in the test corpus without any indicative context. In the same way, if a previously-unseen context appears consistently in the unlabeled corpus before known person names, the tagger should learn that this is a predictive context.

We have adopted a simple learning approach: we take the unlabeled text about which the tagger has greatest confidence in its decisions, tag it, add it to the training set, and retrain the tagger. This process is performed repeatedly to bootstrap ourselves to higher performance. This approach can be used with any supervised-learning tagger that can produce some reliable measure of confidence in its decisions.

4 Baseline Multi-lingual Name Tagger

Our baseline name tagger is based on an HMM that generally follows the Nymble model (Bikel et al, 1997). Then it uses best-first search to generate NBest hypotheses, and also computes the margin – the difference between the log probabilities of the top two hypotheses. This is used as a rough measure of confidence in our name tagging.[1]

In processing Chinese, to take advantage of name structures, we do name structure parsing using an extended HMM which includes a larger number of states (14). This new HMM can handle name prefixes and suffixes, and transliterated foreign names separately. We also augmented the HMM model with a set of post-processing rules to correct some omissions and systematic errors. The name tagger identifies three name types: Person (PER), Organization (ORG) and Geo-political (GPE) entities (locations which are also political units, such as countries, counties, and cities).

5 Two Semi-Supervised Learning Methods for Name Tagging

We have applied this bootstrapping approach to two sources of data: first, to a large corpus of unlabeled data and second, to the test set. To distinguish the two, we shall label the first "bootstrapping" and the second "self-training".

We begin (Sections 5.1 and 5.2) by describing the basic algorithms used for these two processes. We expected that these basic methods would provide a substantial performance boost, but our experiments showed that, for best gain, the additional training data should be related to the target problem, namely, our test set. We present measures to select documents (Section 5.3) and sentences (Section 5.4), and show (in Section 6) the effectiveness of these measures.

5.1 Bootstrapping

We divided the large unlabeled corpus into segments based on news sources and dates in order to: 1) create segments of manageable size; 2) separately evaluate the contribution of each segment (using a labeled development test set) and reject those which do not help; and 3) apply the latest updated best model to each subsequent

[1] We have also used this metric in the context of rescoring of name hypotheses (Ji and Grishman, 2005); Scheffer et al. (2001) used a similar metric for active learning of name tags.

segment. The procedure can be formalized as follows.

1. Select a related set *RelatedC* from a large corpus of unlabeled data with respect to the test set *TestT*, using the document selection method described in section 5.3.

2. Split *RelatedC* into n subsets and mark them $C_1, C_2 \ldots C_n$. Call the updated HMM name tagger *NameM* (initially the baseline tagger), and a development test set *DevT*.

3. For i=1 to n
   (1) Run *NameM* on C_i;

   (2) For each tagged sentence *S* in C_i, if *S* is tagged with high confidence, then keep *S*; otherwise remove *S*;

   (3) Relabel the current name tagger (*NameM*) as *OldNameM*, add C_i to the training data, and retrain the name tagger, producing an updated model *NameM*;

   (4) Run *NameM* on *DevT*; if the performance gets worse, don't use C_i and reset *NameM* = *OldNameM*;

5.2 Self-training

An analogous approach can be used to tag the test set. The basic intuition is that the sentences in which the learner has low confidence may get support from those sentences previously labeled with high confidence.

Initially, we build the baseline name tagger from the labeled examples, then gradually add the most confidently tagged test sentences into the training corpus, and reuse them for the next iteration, until all sentences are labeled. The procedure can be formalized as follows.

1. Cluster the test set *TestT* into n clusters $T_1, T_2, \ldots, T_n$, by collecting document pairs with low cross entropy (described in section 5.3.2) into the same cluster.

2. For i=1 to n
   (1) *NameM* = baseline HMM name tagger;

   (2) While (there are new sentences tagged with confidence higher than a threshold)
   a. Run *NameM* on T_i;
   b. Set an appropriate threshold for margin;
   c. For each tagged sentence *S* in T_i, if *S* is tagged with high confidence, add *S* to the training data;
   d. Retrain the name tagger *NameM* with augmented training data.

At each iteration, we lower the threshold so that about 5% of the sentences (with the largest margin) are added to the training corpus.[2] As an example, this yielded the following gradually improving performance for one English cluster including 7 documents and 190 sentences.

No. of iterations	No. of sentences added	No. of tags changed	F-Measure
0	0	0	91.4
1	37	28	91.9
2	69	22	92.1
3	107	21	92.4
4	128	11	92.6
5	146	9	92.7
6	163	8	92.8
7	178	6	92.8
8	190	0	92.8

Table 1. Incremental Improvement from Self-training (English)

Self-training can be considered a cache model variant, operating across the entire test collection. But it uses confidence measures as weights for each name candidate, and relies on names tagged with high confidence to re-adjust the prediction of the remaining names, while in a cache model, all name candidates are equally weighted for voting (independent of the learner's confidence).

5.3 Unlabeled Document Selection

To further investigate the benefits of using very large corpora in bootstrapping, and also inspired by the gain from the "essence" of self-training, which aims to gradually emphasize the predictions from *related* sentences within the test set, we reconsidered the assumptions of our approach. The bootstrapping method implicitly assumes that the unlabeled data is reliable (not noisy) and uniformly useful, namely:

[2] To be precise, we repeatedly reduce the threshold by 0.1 until an additional 5% or more of the sentences are included; however, if more than an additional 20% of the sentences are captured because many sentences have the same margin, we add back 0.1 to the threshold.

- The unlabeled data supports the acquisition of new names and contexts, to provide new evidence to be incorporated in HMM and reduce the sparse data problem;
- The unlabeled data won't make the old estimates worse by adding too many names whose tags are incorrect, or at least are incorrect in the context of the labeled training data and the test data.

If the unlabeled data is noisy or unrelated to the test data, it can hurt rather than improve the learner's performance on the test set. So it is necessary to coarsely measure the relevance of the unlabeled data to our target test set. We define an IR (information retrieval) - style relevance measure between the test set *TestT* and an unlabeled document *d* as follows.

5.3.1 'Query set' construction

We model the information expected from the unlabeled data by a 'bag of words' technique. We construct a query term set from the test corpus *TestT* to check whether each unlabeled document *d* is useful or not.

- We prefer not to use all the words in *TestT* as key words, since we are only concerned about the distribution of *name candidates*. (Adding off-topic documents may in fact introduce noise into the model). For example, if one document in *TestT* talks about the presidential election in France while *d* talks about the presidential election in the US, they may share many common words such as 'election', 'voting', 'poll', and 'camp', but we would expect more gain from other unlabeled documents talking about the French election, since they may share many name candidates.

- On the other hand it is insufficient to only take the name candidates in the top one hypothesis for each sentence (since we are particularly concerned with tokens which *might* be names but are not so labeled in the top hypothesis).

So our solution is to take all the name candidates in the *top N best* hypotheses for each sentence to construct a query set *Q*.

5.3.2 Cross-entropy Measure

Using *Q*, we compute the cross entropy *H(TestT, d)* between *TestT* and *d* by:

$$H(TestT,d) = -\sum_{x \in Q} prob(x\,|\,TestT) \times \log_2 prob(x\,|\,d)$$

where x is a name candidate in Q, and $prob(x|TestT)$ is the probability (frequency) of x appearing in *TestT* while $prob(x|d)$ is the probability of x in d. If $H(T, d)$ is smaller than a threshold then we consider d a useful unlabeled document[3].

5.4 Sentence Selection

We don't want to add all the tagged sentences in a relevant document to the training corpus because incorrectly tagged or irrelevant sentences can lead to degradation in model performance. The value of larger corpora is partly dependent on how much new information is extracted from each sentence of the unlabeled data compared to the training corpus that we already have.

The following confidence measures were applied to assist the semi-supervised learning algorithm in selecting useful sentences for re-training the model.

5.4.1 Margin to find reliable sentences

For each sentence, we compute the HMM hypothesis margin (the difference in log probabilities) between the first hypothesis and the second hypothesis. We select the sentences with margins larger than a threshold[4] to be added to the training data.

Unfortunately, the margin often comes down to whether a specific word has previously been observed in training; if the system has seen the word, it is certain, if not, it is uncertain. Therefore the sentences with high margins are a mix of interesting and uninteresting samples. We need to apply additional measures to remove the uninteresting ones. On the other hand, we may have confidence in a tagging due to evidence external to the HMM, so we explored measures beyond the HMM margin in order to recover additional sentences.

---

[3] We also tried a single match method, using the query set to find all the relevant documents that include any names belonging to Q, and got approximately the same result as cross-entropy. In addition to this relevance selection, we used one other simple filter: we removed a document if it includes fewer than five names, because it is unlikely to be news.

[4] In bootstrapping, this margin threshold is selected by testing on the development set, to achieve more than 93% F-Measure.

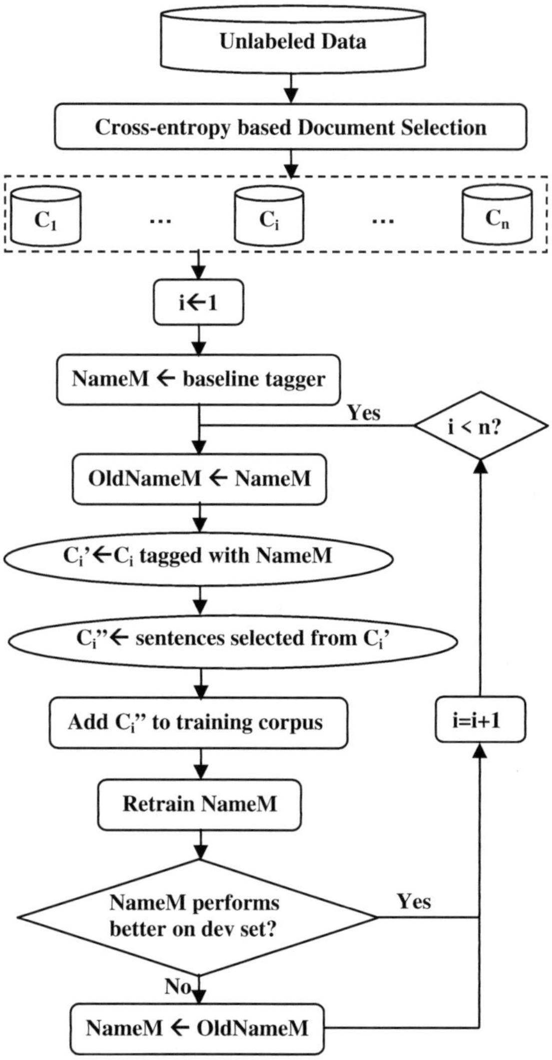

Figure 1. Bootstrapping for Name Tagging

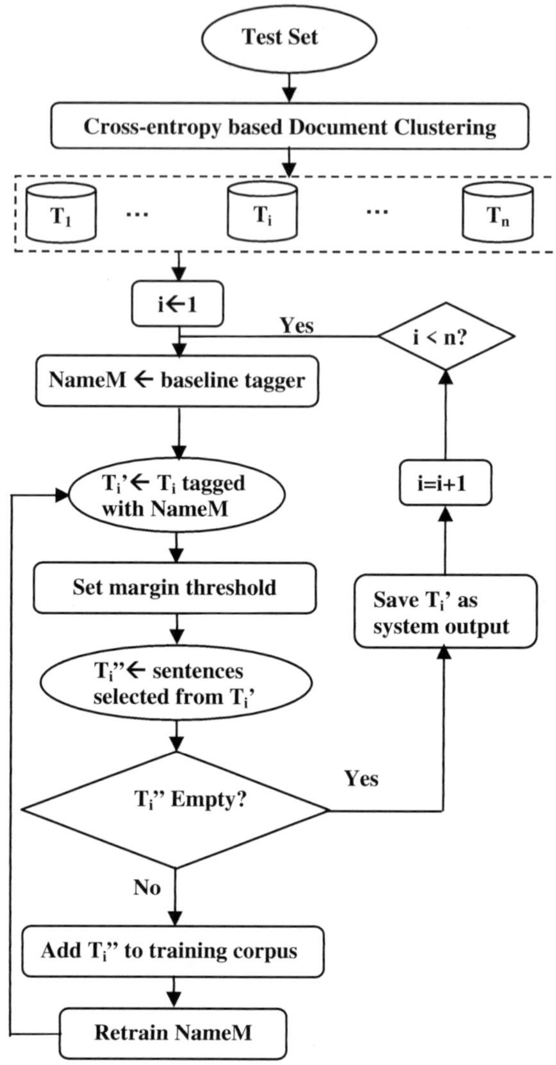

Figure 2. Self-Training for Name Tagging

Data		English	Chinese
Baseline Training data		ACE02,03,04 989,003 words	Beijing Corpus +ACE03,04,05 1,460,648 words
Unlabeled Data	Total	196,494 docs in Mar-Jun of 2003 (69M words) from ACE05 unlabeled data	41061 docs in Nov,Dec of 2000, and Jan of 2001 (25M words) from ACE05 and TDT4 transcripts
	Selected Docs	62584 docs (1,314,148 Sentences)	14,537 docs (222,359 sentences)
	Selected Sentences	290,973 sentences (6,049,378 words)	55,385 sentences (1,128,505 words)
Dev Set		20 ACE04 texts in Oct of 2000	90 ACE05 texts in Oct of 2000
Test Set		20 ACE04 texts in Oct of 2000 and 80 ACE05 texts in Mar-May of 2003 (3093 names, 1205 PERs, 1021GPEs, 867 ORGs)	90 ACE05 texts in Oct of 2000 (3093 names, 1013 PERs, 695 GPEs, 769 ORGs)

Table 2. Data Description

5.4.2 Name coreference to find more reliable sentences

Names introduced in an article are likely to be referred to again, so a name coreferred to by more other names is more likely to have been correctly tagged. In this paper, we use simple coreference resolution between names such as substring matching and name abbreviation resolution.

In the bootstrapping method we apply single-document coreference for each individual unlabeled text. In self-training, in order to further benefit from global contexts, we consider each cluster of relevant texts as one single big document, and then apply cross-document coreference.

Assume *S* is one sentence in the document, and there are *k* names tagged in *S*: $\{N_1, N_2 \ldots\ldots N_k\}$, which are coreferred to by $\{CorefNum_1, CorefNum_2, \ldots CorefNum_k\}$ other names separately. Then we use the following average name coreference count *AveCoref* as a confidence measure for tagging *S*:[5]

$$AveCoref = (\sum_{i=1}^{k} CorefNum_i)/k$$

5.4.3 Name count and sentence length to remove uninteresting sentences

In bootstrapping on unlabeled data, the margin criterion often selects some sentences which are too short or don't include any names. Although they are tagged with high confidence, they may make the model worse if added into the training data (for example, by artificially increasing the probability of non-names). In our experiments we don't use a sentence if it includes fewer than six words, or doesn't include any names.

5.5 Data Flow

We depict the above two semi-supervised learning methods in Figure 1 and Figure 2.

6 Evaluation Results and Discussions

6.1 Data

We evaluated our system on two languages: English and Chinese. Table 2 shows the data used in our experiments.

[5] For the experiments reported here, sentences were selected if *AveCoref* > 3.1 (or 3.1×number of documents for cross-document coreference) *or* the sentence margin exceeded the margin threshold.

We present in section 6.2 – 6.4 the overall performance of precision (P), recall (R) and F-measure (F) for both languages, and also some diagnostic experiment results. For significance testing (using the sign test), we split the test set into 5 folders, 20 texts in each folder of English, and 18 texts in each folder of Chinese.

6.2 Overall Performance

Table 3 and Table 4 present the overall performance[6] by applying the two semi-supervised learning methods, separately and in combination, to our baseline name tagger.

Learner	P	R	F
Baseline	**87.3**	**87.6**	**87.4**
Bootstrapping with data selection	**88.2**	**88.6**	**88.4**
Self-training	**88.1**	**88.4**	**88.2**
Bootstrapping with data selection + Self-training	**89.0**	**89.2**	**89.1**

Table 3. English Name Tagger

Learner	P	R	F
Baseline	**88.2**	**87.6**	**87.9**
Bootstrapping with data selection	**89.8**	**89.5**	**89.6**
Self-training	**89.5**	**88.3**	**88.9**
Bootstrapping with data selection + Self-training	**90.2**	**89.7**	**90.0**

Table 4. Chinese Name Tagger

For English, the overall system achieves a 13.4% relative reduction on the spurious and incorrect tags, and 12.9% reduction in the missing rate. For Chinese, it achieves a 16.9% relative reduction on the spurious and incorrect tags, and 16.9% reduction in the missing rate.[7] For each of the five folders, we found that both bootstrapping and self-training produced an improvement in F score for each folder, and the combination of two methods is always better than each method alone. This allows us to reject the hypothesis that these

[6] Only names which exactly match the key in both extent and type are counted as correct; unlike MUC scoring, no partial credit is given.

[7] The performance achieved should be considered in light of human performance on this task. The ACE keys used for the evaluations were obtained by dual annotation and adjudication. A single annotator, evaluated against the key, scored F=93.6% to 94.1% for English and 92.5% to 92.7% for Chinese. A second key, created independently by dual annotation and adjudication for a small amount of the English data, scored F=96.5% against the original key.

improvements were random at a 95% confidence level.

6.3 Analysis of Bootstrapping

6.3.1 Impact of Data Size

Figure 3 and 4 below show the results as each segment of the unlabeled data is added to the training corpus.

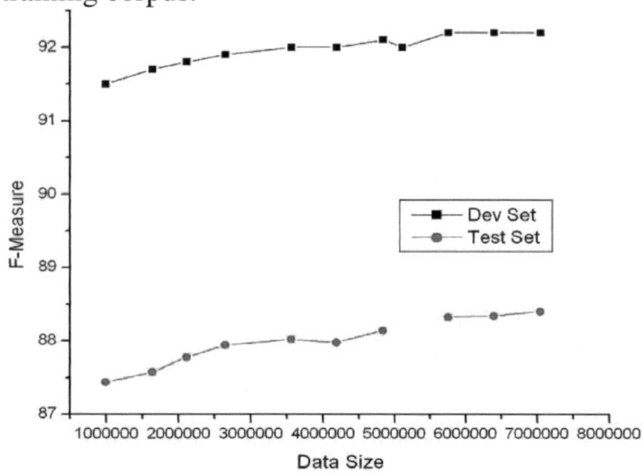

Figure 3. Impact of Data Size (English)

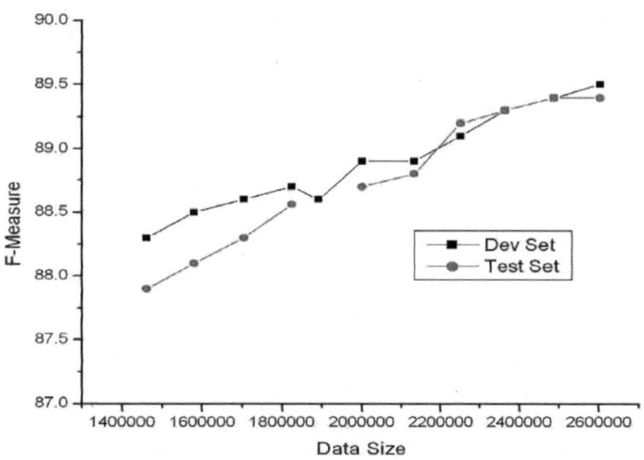

Figure 4. Impact of Data Size (Chinese)

We can see some flattening of the gain at the end, particularly for the larger English corpus, and that some segments do not help to boost the performance (reflected as dips in the Dev Set curve and gaps in the Test Set curve).

6.3.2 Impact of Data Selection

In order to investigate the contribution of document selection in bootstrapping, we performed diagnostic experiments for Chinese, whose results are shown in Table 5. All the bootstrapping tests (rows 2 - 4) use margin for sentence selection; row 4 augments this with the selection methods described in sections 5.4.2 and 5.4.3.

	Learner	P	R	F
(1)	**Baseline**	**88.2**	**87.6**	**87.9**
(2)	**(1) + Bootstrapping**	**88.9**	**88.7**	**88.8**
(3)	**(2) + Document Selection**	**89.3**	**88.9**	**89.1**
(4)	**(3) + Sentence Selection**	**89.8**	**89.5**	**89.6**

Table 5. Impact of Data Selection (Chinese)

Comparing row 2 with row 3, we find that not using document selection, even though it multiplies the size of the corpus, results in 0.3% lower performance (0.3-0.4% loss for each folder). This leads us to conclude that simply relying upon large corpora is not in itself sufficient. Effective use of large corpora demands good confidence measures for document selection to remove off-topic material. By adding sentence selection (results in row 4) the system obtained 0.5% further improvement in F-Measure (0.4-0.7% for each folder). All improvements are statistically significant at the 95% confidence level.

6.4 Analysis of Self-training

We have applied and evaluated different measures to extract high-confidence sentences in self-training. The contributions of these confidence measures to F-Measure are presented in Table 6.

Confidence Measure	English	Chinese
Baseline	**87.4**	**87.9**
Margin	**87.8**	**88.3**
Margin + single-doc name coreference	**88.0**	**88.7**
Margin + cross-doc name coreference	**88.2**	**88.9**

Table 6. Impact of Confidence Measures

It shows that Chinese benefits more from adding name coreference, mainly because there are more coreference links between name abbreviations and full names. And we also can see that the margin is an important measure for both languages. All differences are statistically significant at the 95% confidence level except for the gain using cross-document information for the Chinese name tagging.

7 Conclusions and Future Work

This paper demonstrates the effectiveness of two straightforward semi-supervised learning methods for improving a state-of-art name tagger, and investigates the importance of data selection for this application.

Banko and Brill (2001) suggested that the development of very large training corpora may be central to progress in empirical natural language processing. When using large amounts of unlabeled data, as expected, we did get improvement by using unsupervised bootstrapping. However, exploiting a very large corpus did not by itself produce the greatest performance gain. Rather, we observed that good measures to select relevant unlabeled documents and useful labeled sentences are important.

The work described here complements the active learning research described by (Scheffer et al., 2001). They presented an effective active learning approach that selects "difficult" (small margin) sentences to label by hand and then add to the training set. Our approach selects "easy" sentences – those with large margins – to add automatically to the training set. Combining these methods can magnify the gains possible with active learning.

In the future we plan to try topic identification techniques to select relevant unlabeled documents, and use the downstream information extraction components such as coreference resolution and relation detection to measure the confidence of the tagging for sentences. We are also interested in applying clustering as a pre-processing step for bootstrapping.

Acknowledgment

This material is based upon work supported by the Defense Advanced Research Projects Agency under Contract No. HR0011-06-C-0023, and the National Science Foundation under Grant IIS-00325657. Any opinions, findings and conclusions expressed in this material are those of the authors and do not necessarily reflect the views of the U. S. Government.

References

Rie Ando and Tong Zhang. 2005. A High-Performance Semi-Supervised Learning Methods for Text Chunking. *Proc. ACL2005*. pp. 1-8. Ann Arbor, USA

Michele Banko and Eric Brill. 2001. Scaling to very very large corpora for natural language disambiguation. *Proc. ACL2001*. pp. 26-33. Toulouse, France

David Bean and Ellen Riloff. 2004. Unsupervised Learning of Contextual Role Knowledge for Coreference Resolution. *Proc. HLT-NAACL2004*. pp. 297-304. Boston, USA

Daniel M. Bikel, Scott Miller, Richard Schwartz, and Ralph Weischedel. 1997. Nymble: a high-performance Learning Name-finder. *Proc. Fifth Conf. on Applied Natural Language Processing*. pp.194-201. Washington D.C., USA

Avrim Blum and Tom Mitchell. 1998. Combining Labeled and Unlabeled Data with Co-training. *Proc. of the Workshop on Computational Learning Theory*. Morgan Kaufmann Publishers

Michael Collins and Yoram Singer. 1999. Unsupervised Models for Named Entity Classification. *Proc. of EMNLP/VLC-99.*

James R. Curran and Marc Moens. 2002. Scaling context space. *Proc. ACL 2002*. Philadelphia, USA

James R. Curran. 2002. Ensemble Methods for Automatic Thesaurus Extraction. *Proc. EMNLP 2002*. Philadelphia, USA

James R. Curran and Miles Osborne. 2002. A very very large corpus doesn't always yield reliable estimates. *Proc. ACL 2002 Workshop on Effective Tools and Methodologies for Teaching Natural Language Processing and Computational Linguistics*. Philadelphia, USA

Heng Ji and Ralph Grishman. 2005. Improving Name Tagging by Reference Resolution and Relation Detection. *Proc. ACL2005*. pp. 411-418. Ann Arbor, USA.

Winston Lin, Roman Yangarber and Ralph Grishman. 2003. Bootstrapping Learning of Semantic Classes from Positive and Negative Examples. *Proc. ICML-2003 Workshop on The Continuum from Labeled to Unlabeled Data*. Washington, D.C.

Scott Miller, Jethran Guinness and Alex Zamanian. 2004. Name Tagging with Word Clusters and Discriminative Training. *Proc. HLT-NAACL2004*. pp. 337-342. Boston, USA

Deepak Ravichandran, Patrick Pantel, and Eduard Hovy. 2004. The Terascale Challenge. *Proc. KDD Workshop on Mining for and from the Semantic Web (MSW-04)*. pp. 1-11. Seattle, WA, USA

Ellen Riloff and Rosie Jones. 1999. Learning Dictionaries for Information Extraction by Multi-Level Bootstrapping. *Proc. AAAI/IAAI*

Tobias Scheffer, Christian Decomain, and Stefan Wrobel. 2001. Active Hidden Markov Models for Information Extraction. *Proc. Int'l Symposium on Intelligent Data Analysis (IDA-2001)*.

Tomek Strzalkowski and Jin Wang. 1996. A Self-Learning Universal Concept Spotter. *Proc. COLING.*

LoLo: A System based on Terminology for Multilingual Extraction

Yousif Almas
Department of Computing
University of Surrey
Guildford, Surrey, GU2 7XH, UK
y.almas@surrey.ac.uk

Khurshid Ahmad
Department of Computer Science
Trinity College,
Dublin-2. IRELAND
kahmad@cs.tcd.ie

Abstract

An unsupervised learning method, based on corpus linguistics and special language terminology, is described that can extract time-varying information from text streams. The method is shown to be 'language-independent' in that its use leads to sets of regular-expressions that can be used to extract the information in typologically distinct languages like English and Arabic. The method uses the information related to the distribution of N-grams, for automatically extracting 'meaning bearing' patterns of usage in a training corpus. The analysis of an English news wire corpus (1,720,142 tokens) and Arabic news wire corpus (1,720,154 tokens) show encouraging results.

1 Introduction

One of the recent trends in (adaptive) IE has been motivated by the empirical argument that annotated corpora, either annotated automatically or annotated manually, can provide sufficient information for creating the knowledge base of an IE system (McLernon and Kushmerick, 2006). Another equally important trend is to use manually selected seed patterns to initiate learning: In turn, active-training methods use seed patterns to learn new related patterns from unannotated corpora. Many of the adaptive IE systems rely on the existing part-of-speech (POS) taggers (Debnath and Giles, 2005) and/or syntactic parsers (Stevenson and Greenwood, 2005) for analysing and annotating text corpora. The use of corpora in IE, especially adaptive IE, should, in principle, alleviate the need for manually creating the rules for information extraction.

The successful use of POS/syntactic taggers is dependent on the availability of the knowledge of (natural) language used by the authors of documents in a given corpus. There is a wealth of POS taggers and parsers available for English language, as it has been the most widely used language in computational linguistics. However, this is not the case for strategically important languages like Arabic and Chinese; to start with, in Chinese one does not have the luxury of separating word-tokens by a white space and in Arabic complex rules are required to identify morphemes compared to English. The development of segmentation programs in these languages has certainly helped (Gao et al., 2005; Habash and Rambow, 2005). More work is needed in understanding these languages such that the knowledge thus derived can be used to power taggers and parsers.

Typically, IE systems are used to analyse news wire corpora, telephone conversations, and more recently in bio-informatics. The first two systems deal with language of everyday communications –the *general language*- whereas bio-informatics deals with a specialist domain and has its own 'special language'. English special languages, for example *languages of law, commerce, finance, science & technology*, each have a limited vocabulary and idiosyncratic syntactic structures when compared with English used in an everyday context. The same is true of German, French, Russian, Chinese, Arabic or Hindi. It appears that few works, if any, take advantage of the properties of special language to build IE systems.

Our objective is to use methods and techniques of IE in the automatic analysis of specialist news that streams in such a way that information extracted at an earlier period of time may be contradicted or reinforced by information extracted at a later time. The *impact of news* on financial and commodity markets is of consider-

Proceedings of the Workshop on Information Extraction Beyond The Document, pages 56–65,
Sydney, July 2006.

able import and is often called *sentiment analysis*. The prefix 'sentiment' is used to distinguish this kind of analysis from the more quantitative analysis of assets (called fundamental analysis) and that of price movements (called technical analysis). There is a great deal of discussion in financial economics, econometrics, and in the newly emergent discipline of *investor psychology* about the impact of 'good' and 'bad' news on the behaviour of both investors and brokers. Three Nobel Prizes have been awarded on the impact of market (trader and investor) sentiment on the value of shares, currencies, derivatives and other financial instruments (Shiller, 2000). Financial news, in addition to e-mails and blogs, has contributed to the catastrophic failures of major trading institutions (Mackenzie, 2000; Hardie & Mackenzie, 2005).

One of the key proponents of *news impact analysis* is the Economics Nobel Laureate Robert Engle who has written about asymmetry of information in a market – the brokers have more knowledge than any given individual, rumours have different impact on different actors in the market. Engle's statistical analysis suggests that the 'bad' news has longer lasting effect than 'good' news (Engle, 1993). Usually, sentiment analysis is carried out using news *proxies* which include dates/times and the names of agencies releasing key items of financial data (Anderson et al., 2002) or data like the age of a firm, its number of initial public offerings, return on investment, etc. These proxies are then regressed with share, currency or commodity prices. News impact analysis is moving into its next phase where the text of news is analysed albeit to a limited extent (Cutler et al., 1989; Chan, 2003). The analysis sometimes looks at the frequency distribution of pre-specified keywords –directional metaphors like *rose/fall, up/down,* health metaphors like *anaemic/healthy* and animal metaphors like *bullish/bearish.* A system is trained to correlate and to *learn* the changes in distribution of the prescribed metaphorical keywords, together with names of organisations, to the changes in the value of financial instruments (Seo et al., 2002; Omrane et al., 2005; Koppel and Shtrimberg 2004).

We are attempting to create a language-informed framework for news impact analysis using techniques of corpus linguistics and special language analysis. The purpose is to automatically extract patterns from a corpus of domain specific texts without prescribing the metaphorical keywords and organisation names. This, we believe, can be achieved by looking at the *lexical signature* of a specialist domain and extracting collocational patterns of the individual items of the lexical signature. The lexical signature includes key vocabulary items of the domain and names of people, places and things in the domain. There are instances in the part-of-speech tagging literature (Brill, 1993) and in IE where a corpus is used and words within a grammatical category help to extract rules and patterns comprising essential information about a domain or topic (Wilks, 1998; Yangarber, 2003). Brill, Wilks and Yangarber *induce* grammars of a universal kind: we focus on inducing a local grammar that deals with the patterning of the items in the signature. Note that in all these cases of grammar induction the intuition of the grammar builder plays a critical part whether it be in the choice of syntactic transformation rules (Brill 1993), or in choosing sense taggers and implicitly semantic rules (Wilks, 1998; Ciravegna and Wilks, 2003), or in choosing user supplied seed patterns (Yangarber, 2003). Most of the work in grammar induction is focussed on English or typologically similar languages. We have deliberately chosen typologically different languages (English and Arabic) to evaluate the extent to which our method of 'grammar induction' is language independent.

We describe a method for building domain specific IE systems: the patterns used to extract domain specific information are the N-gram collocation patterns of domain specific terms. The patterns are extracted from un-annotated domain-specific text corpora. We show how one can analyse the N-gram patterns and render them as *regular expressions.*

The thesaurus used to identify domain specific words is itself constructed automatically from a (training) special-language corpus. The frequency distribution of domain specific terms in a special language corpus shows characteristic differences from the distribution of the same terms in a general language corpus. There is little or no difference in the distribution of the so-called grammatical or closed class terms in a special and a general language corpus.

Furthermore, amongst the domain specific terms, a few tend to dominate the frequency distribution – the so-called lexical signature of a domain. These signature terms are used as nucleates for compound terms in a domain. The occurrence of the signature terms, either on their own or in a compound or a phrase, is equally idiosyncratic in that these dominant single or compound terms co-occur more frequently with one set of words than with others. The behaviour of signature terms appears to be governed by a grammar that is local to the specialism and is not elsewhere in the general language (Harris, 1991); *local grammar* is used in general language for telling times and dates in metaphorical expressions (Gross, 1997), and in the lexicography for describing the *language of definitions* of lemmas in a lexicon (Barnbrook and Sinclair, 1996; Barnbrook, 2002). The local grammar approach, rooted in the lexical signature of a given domain can be used to extract 'sentiment' bearing sentences in financial markets (Ahmad el al., 2006) or in the description of work in a scientific laboratory (Ahmad & Al-Sayed, 2005).

We introduce a system that can help in building domain specific IE systems in English and languages that are typologically distinct from English, specifically Arabic. The development of *LoLo* was inspired by Engle's pioneering work in econometrics where news impact analysis is regarded as critical to the analysis of market movement: however much of the work in financial economics relates to the correlation of the timings of news announcements rather than the content of the news stream (Ahmad et al., 2006).

LoLo can manage a corpus and extract key terms. Given the keyword list, the system then identifies collocates and selects significant collocates on well defined statistical criterion (Smadja, 1994). Finally, local grammar rules are identified and an IE system is created.

LoLo has been used to build a local grammar to extract 'sentiment' or key (changing) market events in English and in Arabic from unseen texts. The system can help visualise the distribution of extracted patterns synchronised with the movement of financial markets.

IE systems need to be adaptive, as the specialisms in particular and the world in general is changing rapidly and this change is usually reflected in language use. There is an equally important need to build cross language IE systems as information may be in different languages. The lexically-motivated approach we describe in this paper responds to the need for an adaptive, cross domain and cross language IE systems.

2 Method

For the extraction of local grammar from a corpus of special language texts it is important to focus on the keywords. The patterns in which the keywords are embedded are assumed to comprise the principal elements of a subject specific local grammar.

The manner in which we derive the local grammar is shown in the algorithm below (Figure 1).

ALGORITHM: DISCOVER LOCAL GRAMMAR

1. **SELECT** *a special language corpus* (S_L, *comprising* $N_{special}$ *words and vocabulary* $V_{Special}$).
   - i. **USE** *a frequency list of single words from a corpus of texts used in day-to-day communications* (S_G *comprising* $N_{general}$ *words and vocabulary* $V_{general}$) – *for example, the British National Corpus for the English language:*
     $$F_{general}:=\{f(w_1), f(w_2), f(w_3) \ldots \ldots f_{V_{general}}\}$$
   - ii. **CREATE** *a frequency ordered list of words in* S_L *texts is computed*
     $$F_{special}:=\{f(w_1), f(w_2), f(w_3) \ldots \ldots \ldots\}$$
   - iii. **COMPUTE** *the differences in the distribution of the same words in the two different corpora is computed using the in* S_G *and* S_L:
     $$Weirdness\ (w_i) = f(w_i)special/f(w_i)general * N_{general}/N_{special}$$
   - iv. **CALCULATE** *z-score for the* $F_{speical}$
     $$zf(w_i)=(f(w_i)-f_{av\_special})/\sigma_{special}$$
2. **CREATE** *KEY a set of* N_{key} *keywords ordered according to the magnitude of the two z-scores*
   $$KEY:=\{key_1, key_2, key_3 \ldots \ldots key_{Nkey})$$
   $$\text{such that } z(f_{keyi})\ \&\ z(weridness_{keyi}) > 1$$
   - i. **EXTRACT** *collocates of each Key in* S_L *over a window of* ***M*** *word neighbourhood.*
   - ii. **COMPUTE** *the strength of collocation using three measures due to Smadja (1994):*
     U-score, k, and z-score
   - iii. **EXTRACT** *sentences in the corpus that comprise highly collocating key-words* $((U, k_o, k_1) >= (10, 1, 1)) \rightarrow$
   - iv. **FORM** *Corpus* S_L'
     - a. *For each Sentence*$_i$ *in* $S_{L'}$:
     - b. **COMPUTE** *the frequency of every word in Sentence*$_i$.
     - c. **REPLACE** *words with frequency less than a threshold value* ($f_{threshold}$) *by a place marker #;*
     - d. **FOR** *more than one contiguous place marker, use**
3. **GENERATE** *trigrams in* $S_{L'}$; *note frequency of each trigram together with its position in the sentences:*
   - i. **FIND** *all the longest possible contiguous trigrams across all sentences in SL' and note their frequency*
   - ii. **ORDER** *the (contiguous) trigrams according to frequency of occurrence*
   - iii. **(CONTIGUOUS) TRIGRAMS** *with frequency above a threshold form* **THE LOCAL GRAMMAR**

Figure 1. Algorithm for the acquisition of local-grammar patterns.

Briefly, given a specialist corpus (S_L), keywords are identified, and collocates of the keywords are extracted. Sentences containing key collocates are then used to construct a sub-corpus (S_L'). The sub-corpus S_L' is then analyzed and trigrams above a frequency threshold in the sub-corpus are extracted; the position of the trigrams in each of the sentences is also noted. The sub-corpus is searched again for contiguous trigrams across the sentences: The sentences are analyzed for the existence of the trigrams in the correct position – if a trigram that, for example, is noted for its frequency as a sentence initial position, is found to co-occur with another frequent trigram that exists at the next position, then the two trigrams will be deemed to form a pattern.

This process is continued until all the trigrams in the sentence are matched with the significant trigrams.

The local grammar then comprises significant contiguous trigrams that are found. These domain specific patterns, extracted from the specialist corpus S_L' (and its constituent sub-corpus) are then used to extract similar patterns and information from a test corpus to validate the patterns thus found in the training corpus. Following is a demonstration of how the algorithm works using English and Arabic texts.

2.1 Extracting Patterns in English

We present an analysis of a corpus of financial news wire texts: 1204 news report produced by Reuters UK Financial News comprising 431,850 tokens. One of the frequent words in the corpus is *percent*– 3622 occurrences, a relative frequency of 0.0084%. When the frequency of this keyword is looked up in the British National Corpus (100 million words), it was found that *percent* is 287 times more frequent in the financial corpus than in the British National Corpus – this ratio is sometimes termed *weirdness* (of special language); the weirdness of grammatical words *the* and *to* is unity as these tokens are distributed with the same (relative) frequency in Reuters Financial and the BNC. The z-score computed using the frequency of the token in the Reuters Financial is 12.64: the distribution of *percent* is 12 standard deviations above the mean of all words in the financial corpus. (The z-score computed for weirdness is positive as well). The heuristic here is this: a token is a candidate *keyword* if both its z-scores are greater than a small positive number. So *percent* -most frequent token with frequency and weirdness z-score over zero- *was* accepted as a keyword.

The collocates of the keyword *percent* were then extracted by using mutual information statistics presented by Smadja (1994). A collocate in this terminology can be anywhere in the vicinity of +/- N-words. The frequency at each neighbourhood is calculated and then used to compute the 'peaks' in the histogram formed by the neighbourhood frequencies and the strength of the collocation calculated on a similar basis. The keyword generally collocates with certain words that have frequencies higher than itself – the *upward collocates*- and collocates with certain words that have lesser frequency – the *downwards collocates* (These terms were coined by John Sinclair). Upwards collocates are usually grammatical words and downwards collocates are lexical words – nouns, adjectives- and hence the downwards collocates are treated as candidate compound words. There were 46 collocates of *percent* in our corpus – 34 *downwards* collocates and 12 *upwards* collocates. A selection of 5 downwards and upwards are shown in Table 1 and 2 respectively.

Collocate	Frequency	U-score	k-score
shares	1150	1047	3.01
rose	514	2961	2.43
year	2046	396	2.40
profit	1106	263	1.65
down	486	996	1.40

Table 1. Downward collocates of *percent* in a corpus of 431,850 words.

Collocate	Frequency	U-score	k-score
the	23157	6744	14.40
to	12190	7230	10.29
in	9768	4941	8.49
a	10657	3024	8.44
of	10123	3957	8.24

Table 2. Upward collocates of *percent* in a corpus of 431,850 words.

The financial texts comprise a large number of numerals (integers and decimals) and these we will denote as <no>. The numerals collocate strongly with *percent* for obvious reasons. The collocates are then used to extract trigrams comprising the collocates that occur at particular positions in the various sentences of our corpus:

Token A	Token B	Token C	Freq	Position
<no>	**percent**	and	16	1
rose	<no>	**percent**	18	1
<no>	**percent**	after	23	2
<no>	**percent**	of	47	2
<no>	**percent**	rise	11	2

Table 3. Trigrams of *percent*.

There are many other frequent patterns where the frequency of individual tokens is quite low but at least one member of the trigram has higher frequency: such low frequency tokens are omitted and marked by the (#) symbol. All the trigrams containing such tokens with at least two others are used to extract other significant trigrams. Sometimes more than one low frequency tokens precede or succeed high frequency tokens and they are denoted by the symbol (*) as shown in Table 4. The search for contiguous trigrams leads to larger and more complex patterns, Table 5 provides some examples.

Token A	Token B	Token C	Freq	Position
rose	<no>	**percent**	18	1
#	<no>	**percent**	29	2
#	shares	were	10	2
*	<no>	**percent**	57	2
<no>	**percent**	#	24	2

Table 4. Trigrams of *percent* with omitted low frequency words (denoted as * for multiple tokens and # for a single token).

Local Grammar Patterns	Freq
<s> the * <no> **percent**	28
<s> * rose <no> **percent**	26
<s> # shares # <no> **percent**	22
<s> * fell <no> **percent**	20
<s> * <no> **percent**	18
<s> # shares were up <no> **percent** at	17

Table 5. Some of top patterns of *percent* (<s> identifies a sentence boundary).

2.2 Extracting Patterns in Arabic

Arabic is written from right to left and its writing system does not employ capitalization. The language is highly inflected compared to English; words are generated using a root-and-pattern morphology. Prefixes and suffixes can be attached to the morphological patterns for grammatical purposes. For example, the grammatical conjunction "and" in Arabic is attached to the beginning of the following word. Words are also sensitive to the gender and number they refer to and their lexical structure change accordingly. As a result, more word types can be found in Arabic corpora compared to English of same size and type. Short vowels which are represented as marks in Arabic are also omitted from usual Arabic texts resulting in some words having same lexical structures but different semantics.

These grammatical and lexical features of Arabic cause more complexity and ambiguity, especially for NLP systems designed for thorough processing of Arabic texts compared to English. A shallow and statistical approach for IE using texts of specialism can be useful to abstract many complexities of Arabic texts.

Given a 431,563 word corpus comprising 2559 texts of Reuters Arabic Financial News and the same thresholds we used with the English corpus, *percent* (*al-meaa*, المئة) is again the most frequent term with frequency and weirdness z-score greater than zero. It has 3125 occurrences (0.0072%), a frequency z-score of 19.03 and a weirdness of 76 compared against our Modern Standard Arabic Corpus (MSAC).

There were 31 collocates of *percent*; 7 upwards and 23 downwards. The downwards collocates of *percent* appear to collocate with names of instruments i.e. *shares* and *indices* (Table 6).

The upwards collocate are with the so-called closed class words as in English like *in, on* and *that* (Table 7).

Collocate	Freq	U-score	k-score
by-a-ratio (*be-nesba*, بنسبة)	1257	39191	7.87
point (*noqta*, نقطة)	1167	9946	6.44
the-year (*al-aam*, العام)	1753	344	3.34
index (*moasher*, مؤشر)	1130	409	2.55
million (*milyoon*, مليون)	2281	600	2.32
share (*saham*, سهم)	705	206	1.84

Table 6. Downward collocates of *percent* (*al-meaa*, المئة).

Collocate	Freq	U-score	k-score
in (*fee*, في)	21236	434756	40.99
to (*ela*, الى)	3339	25145	9.81
from (*min*, من)	10344	4682	9.58
on (*ala*, على)	5275	117	3.10
that (*ann*, ان)	5130	260	2.65

Table 7. Upward collocates of *percent* (*almeaa*, المئة).

Using the same thresholds the trigrams (Table 8) appear to be different from the English trigrams in that the words of movement are not included here – this is because Arabic has a richer morphological system compared to English and Financial Arabic is not as standardised as Financial English: however, it will not be difficult to train the system to recognise the variants of *rose* and *fell* in Financial Arabic. Table 9 lists some of the patterns.

Token A	Token B	Token C	Freq	Position
<no>	in (*fee*,في)	**percent** (*al-meaa*,المئة)	197	1
in (*fee*,في)	**percent** (*al-meaa*,المئة)	*	39	1
in (*fee*,في)	**percent** (*al-meaa*,المئة)	to (*ela*, الى)	22	2
percent (*al-meaa*,المئة)	to (*ela*, الى)	<no>	21	3
#	in (*fee*,في)	**percent** (*al-meaa*,المئة)	66	4

Table 8. Trigrams of *percent* (*almeaa*, المئة).

Local Grammar Patterns	Freq
<s> * <no> في المئة * percent in	34
<s> * بنسبة <no> في المئة الى <no> *to percent in by-a-ratio*	23
<s> # سهم # <no> في المئة *percent in share*	21
<s> # مؤشر # الاوسع نطاقا بنسبة <no> في المئة الى <no> نقطة <s/> *point to percent in by-ratio wider index*	18
مؤشر * <no> نقطة أي <no> في المئة الى <no> نقطة <s/> *point to percent in namely point index*	16
في * يوم # بنسبة <no> في المئة مع * *with percent in by-ratio day in*	10

Table 9. Some patterns of *percent* (*almeaa*, المئة).

3 Experimental Results

We have argued that a method that is focused on frequency at the lexical level(s) of linguistic description – single words, compounds, and N-grams- will perhaps lead to patterns that are idiosyncratic of a specialist domain without recourse to a thesaurus. There are a number of linguistic methods – that focus on syntactic and semantic level of description which might be of equal or better use.

In order to show the effectiveness of our method we apply it to sentiment analysis – an analysis that attempts to extract qualitative opinion expressed about a range of human and natural artefacts – films, cars, financial instruments for instance. Broadly speaking, sentiments in financial markets relate to the 'rise' and 'fall' of financial instruments (shares, currencies, commodities and energy prices): inextricably these sentiments relate to change in the prices of the instruments. In both English and Arabic, we have found that *percent* or equivalent is a keyword and trigrams and longer N-grams embedded with this keyword relate to metaphorical movement words– *up, down, rise, fall*. However, in English this association is further contextualised with other keywords – *shares, stocks*- and in Arabic the contextualisation is with shares and the principal commodity of many Arab states economies – *oil*. Our system 'discovered' both by following a lexical level of linguistic description.

For each of the two languages of interest to us, we have created 1.72 million token corpora. Each corpus was then divided into two (roughly) equal sized sub corpora: training corpus and testing corpus; the testing corpus is sub-divided into two testing corpora $Test_1$ and $Test_2$ (Table 10). First, we extract patterns from the Training Corpus using the *discover local grammar* algorithm (Figure 1) and also from $Test_1$. Next, the $Training_1$ and $Test_1$ corpora are merged and patterns extracted from the merged corpus. The intuition we have is that as the size of the corpus is increased the patterns extracted from a smaller sized corpus will be elaborated: some of the patterns that are idiosyncratic of the smaller sized corpus will become statistically insignificant and hence will be ignored. The conventional way of testing would have been to see how many patterns discovered in the training corpus are found in the testing corpora; we are quantifying these results currently. In the following we describe an initial test of our method after introducing *LoLo*.

Corpus	English		Arabic	
	Texts	Tokens	Texts	Tokens
$Training_1$	2408	861,492	5118	860,020
$Test_1$	1204	431,850	2559	431,563
$Training_2$ ($Training_1$+$Test_1$)	3612	1,293,342	7677	1,293,342
$Test_2$	1204	426,800	2559	428,571
Total	**4816**	**1,720,142**	**10,236**	**1,720,154**

Table 10. Training and testing corpora used in our experiments.

3.1 LoLo

*LoLo (*stands for *Local-Grammar for Learning Terminology* and means 'pearl' in Arabic*)* is developed using the .NET platform. It contains four components summarised in Table 11.

Component	Functionality
CORPUS ANALYSER	Discover domain specific extraction patterns
RULES EDITOR	Group, label and evaluate patterns and slots
INFORMATION EXTRACTOR	Extract information
INFORMATION VISUALISER	Visualise patterns over time

Table 11. Summary of *LoLo's* components.

The various components of *LoLo* –the *Analyser, Editor*, *Extractor* and the *Visualiser*, can be used to extract and present patterns; the system has utilities to change script and the direction of writing (Arabic is right-to-left and English left-to-right). Table 12 is an exemplar output from *LoLo:* "rise in profit" event patterns expressed similarly in English and Arabic financial news headlines found by the *Corpus Analyser*.

English	* profit up <no> percent
Arabic	ارتفاع أرباح * <no> في المئة *percent in profit rise (up)*

Table 12. "Rise in profit" patterns in Arabic and English where the * usually comprises names of organisations or enterprises.

The pattern acquisition algorithm presented earlier is implemented in the *Corpus Analyser* component, which is the focus of this paper. It can be used for discovering frequent patterns in corpora. The user has the option to filter smaller patterns contained in larger ones and to mine for interrupted or non-interrupted patterns. It can also distinguish between single word and multi word slots.

Before mining for patterns, a corpus preprocessor routine performs a few operations to improve the pattern discovery. It identifies any punctuation marks attached to the words and separates them. it also identifies the sentences boundaries and converts all the numerical tokens to one tag "<no>" as numbers can be part of some patterns, especially in the domain of financial news.

The *Rules Editor* is at its initial stages of development, currently it can export the extraction patterns discovered by the *Corpus Analyser* as *regular expressions*.

A time-stamped corpus can be visualised using the *Information Visualiser*. The *Visualiser* can display a time-series that shows how the extracted events emerge, repeat and fade over time in relation to other events or imported time series i.e. of financial instruments. This can be useful for analysing any relations between different events or detecting trends in one or more corpora or with other time-series.

LoLo facilitates other corpus and computational linguistics tasks as well, including generating concordances and finding collocations from texts encoded in UTF-8. This is particularly useful for Arabic and languages using the Arabic writing system like Persian and Urdu which lack such resources.

3.2 Training and Testing

3.2.1 English

We consider the English Training$_1$ corpus first. We extracted the significant collocates of all the high frequency/high weirdness words, where 'high' defined using the associated z-scores, in the training corpus. Trigrams were then extracted and high frequency trigrams were chosen and all sentences comprising the trigrams were used to form a (training) sub corpus. The sub-corpus was then analysed for extracting the local grammar.

The 10 high frequency N-grams extracted automatically from the Training$_1$ Corpus (861,492) are listed in Table 13. The Test$_1$ corpus has most of the trigrams in the Training$_1$ corpus, particularly some of the larger N-grams (Table 14).

Rank	Top 10 patterns comprising 'percent'	Freq
1	<s> the * <no> percent	45
2	<s> the * was up <no> percent at <no>, <no> </s>	33
3	<s> * <no> percent #, <no> </s>	24
4	<s> * up <no> percent	21
5	<s> the * was down <no> percent at <no> , <no> </s>	19
6	<s> * <no> percent after	18
6	<s> * <no> percent to <no> , <no> yen	18
7	<s>, # shares were up <no> percent at <no>	17
8	<s> shares in * <no> percent	15
9	<s> * rose <no> percent to <no>	14
10	<s> # shares rose <no> percent to <no>	13
10	<s> fell <no> percent to <no>	13

Table 13. Patterns of *percent* extracted from Training$_1$ corpus.

Patterns	Freq
<s> # shares # <no> percent	22
<s> shares in * <no> percent	13
<s> # shares were up <no> percent at	17

Table 14. Patterns of *percent* extracted from Test$_1$ corpus found as sub-patterns in Training$_1$.

We then merged the Training$_1$ and Test$_1$ corpora together and created Training$_2$ corpus comprising of 3612 texts and 1,293,342 tokens. The Algorithm was executed on the merged corpus and a new set of patterns were extracted, in particular the most frequent pattern in the Training$_1$ Corpus (*<s> the * <no> percent*), was elaborated by the Algorithm as well as those patterns shown in Table 15.

Training$_1$ Corpus	Freq	Training$_2$ Corpus	Freq
<s> the * was down <no> percent at <no> , <no> </s>	19	<s> the * **index** was down <no> percent at <no> , <no> </s>	23
<s> the * was up <no> percent at <no>, <no> </s>	33	<s> the * **index** was up <no> percent at <no> , <no> </s>	34

Table 15. Comparison between two patterns in Training$_1$ and Training$_2$ corpora.

The patterns related to the collocations of shares and percent from Training$_1$ were preserved in Training$_2$. The test on Test$_2$ corpus showed similar results: the smaller N-grams related to the movement of instruments were similar to the Test$_1$ Corpus. The analysis of Arabic texts is shown below with similar results.

3.2.2 Arabic

Some of frequent N-grams extracted automatically from the Training$_1$ Arabic corpus (860,020) are shown in Table 16. Similar to the English corpora the Test$_1$ Arabic corpus has most of the trigrams in the Training$_1$ Corpus and some larger N-grams(Table 17).

Rank	Top 10 patterns comprising 'percent'	Freq
1	<s> * <no> في السنة * *percent in*	35
2	* في * بنسبة <no> في المئة *percent in by-ratio in*	31
3	* <no> نقطة بنسبة <no> في المئة الى <no> نقطة <s/> *point to percent in by-ratio point*	28
4	<s> * في المئة في * *in percent in*	24
4	<s> * بنسبة <no> في المئة الى <no> *to percent in by-ratio*	24
5	* في * الى <no> في المئة *percent in to in*	21
5	<s># مؤشر * نطاقا بنسبة<no>في المئة الى <no>نقطة<s/> *point to percent in by-ratio zone index*	21

Table 16. Patterns of *percent* (*almeaa*, المئة) extracted from Training$_1$ Arabic corpus.

Patterns	Freq
* بنسبة <no> في المئة # *percent in by-ratio*	10
* بنسبة <no> في المئة في *in percent in by-ratio*	10
<s> * بنسبة <no> في المئة * *percent in by-ratio*	11

Table 17. Patterns of *percent* (*almeaa*, المئة) extracted from Test$_1$ Arabic corpus found as sub-patterns in Training$_1$.

After merging the Training$_1$ and Test$_1$ Arabic corpora together into a corpus of 7677 texts and 1,293,342 tokens, new set of patterns were extracted as well. Some of the frequent patterns in the training corpus were elaborated more as well like the pattern shown in Table 18 where the token *and-rise* (*wa-ertifaa*, وارتفع) was added to the pattern.

Training$_1$ Corpus	**Freq**	**Training$_2$ Corpus**	**Freq**
<s> # مؤشر # الاوسع نطاقا بنسبة <no> في المئة الى <no> نقطة </s>	13	<s> **وارتفع** مؤشر # الاوسع نطاقا بنسبة <no> في المئة الى <no> نقطة </s>	17

Table 18. Comparison between two patterns in Training$_1$ and Training$_2$ Arabic corpora.

4 Evaluation

We have used the *Rules Editor* and the *Information Extractor* to evaluate the patterns on a corpus comprising 2408 texts and 858,650 tokens created by merging Test$_1$ and Test$_2$ corpora. The Arabic evaluation corpus comprised 5118 texts and 860,134 tokens. The N-gram pattern extractor (where N > 4) showed considerable promise in that who or what went up/or down was unambiguously extracted from the English test corpus using patterns generated through the training corpus. Initial results show high precision with the longer N-grams in English (Table 19) and Arabic (Table 20).

Pattern	Precision
<ORG> shares were down <no> percent at <no>	100% (13/13)
<Movement> <no> percent to <no> , <no> yen	100% (17/17)
the **<Index>** was up <no> percent at <no> , <no>	92% (11/12)
<ORG> shares # up <no> percent at	88% (30/34)

Table 19. Patterns with high precision (English).

Pattern	Precision
مؤشر **<Index>** <no> نقطة أي <no> في المئة الى <no> نقطة *point to percent in viz point index*	100% (42/42)
مؤشر **<Index>** لاسهم # <no> نقطة # <no> في المئة *percent in point for-shares index*	100% (27/27)
<Movement> مؤشر **<Index>**الاوسع نطاقا بنسبة <no> في المئة الى<no>نقطة *point to percent in by-ratio zone wider index*	97% (33/34)
<Movement> مؤشر **<Index>** نطاقا <no> في المئة الى <no> نقطة *point to percent in zone index*	77% (27/35)

Table 20. Patterns with high precision (Arabic).

However, some patterns return many extracted information that require trimming. For example many organizations names are extracted in Arabic using the pattern shown in table 21 but they usually have the word by-a-ratio (*be-nesba*, بنسبة) attached at the end resulting in low precision.

Pattern	Precision
<ORG> rose <no> percent to <no>	36% (5/14)
<Movement> سهم شركة **<ORG>** <no> في المئة *percent in company share*	30% (25/83)

Table 21. Patterns with low precision in English and Arabic

Because we have used the same training thresholds for English and Arabic, the patterns in Arabic appeared without the motion words. However the system can extract these words along with the org/instrument/index names because they appear frequently as slots in the patterns.

The N-gram patterns (when $N \leq 4$) show poor results in that either such patterns found in the training corpus are not found in the test corpus, or the patterns retrieved from test corpora are at semantic variance with the same pattern in the training corpus. This suggests that there is an optimal length of individual patterns in our local grammar.

5 Afterword

The patterns extracted from the English (and Arabic) corpora confirm to an extent the view of the proponents of *local grammar,* of a special language, that there are certain words (in our case *percent, shares, index*) that appear to have a specific grammatical category in the sense that the neighbourhood of these words is occupied by a small number of other words (*up, down, fall, rise, <no>* for instance). If we were to apply the grammars typically used in part-of-speech taggers and syntactic parsing in general, the idiosyncratic behaviour of the pivotal keywords in specialist language does not become apparent: the pivotal keywords are regarded as noun phrases and the association of these phrases is with other general categories of verb phrase, adjectival phrase and adverbial phrase.

The patterns we have extracted could have been extracted with the help of a thesaurus. And, this is the question which is critical to us: how to create and maintain a thesaurus within a domain. This is illustrated in a small way by our experiment on the Training$_1$ corpus where the term *index* was not statistically significant for it to appear in the trigrams that populate the local grammar. However, in Training$_2$, the larger corpus did contain significant frequency of the term *index* for it to make into a pattern of its own. Furthermore, many of the patterns in Training$_1$ persisted in Training$_2$. Smaller N-grams persist as well in the various Training and Test corpora – these patterns in themselves act like units around which other trigrams nucleate.

The evaluation of our Algorithm is still continuing and we are in the process of setting up experiments with human volunteers, especially those with some knowledge of financial matters to evaluate the output of *LoLo*. We intend to use information retrieval metrics of recall and the various $F\beta$ measures.

The local grammar movement has made erratic progress since its inception in the 1960's. Now, with the advent of accessible computers with substantive memories, with the advent of the Internet and the concomitant treasure of multi-lingual text deposits and text streams, one can explore the use of such grammars in addressing the major challenges in information extraction.

Reference

Ahmad, Khurshid. and Al-Sayed, Rafif. (2005) Community of Practice and the Special Language 'Ground'. In (Eds.) Clarke, S and Coakes, E. *Encyclopaedia of Knowledge Management and Community of Practice*. Hershey (PA): The Idea Group Reference.

Ahmad, Khurshid., Cheng, David. and Almas, Yousif. (2006) 'Multi-lingual Sentiment Analysis of Financial News Streams.' In *Proc. of the 1st International Conference on Grid in Finance*, Palermo.

Andersen, Torben., Bollerslev, Tim., Diebold, Francis, and Vega, Clara. (2002). 'Micro effects of macro announcements: Real Time Price Discovery in Foreign Exchange'. National Bureau of Economic Research Working Paper 8959. (Available at http://www.nber.org/papers/w8959).

Barnbrook, Geoffrey. and Sinclair, John McH. (1996) 'Parsing Cobuild Entries'. In (Eds.) John McH. Sinclair, Martin Hoelter & Carol Peters. *The Languages of Definition: the Formalization of Dictionary Definitions for Natural Language Processing*: Luxembourg: Office for Official Publications of the European Communities, pp 13-58.

Barnbrook, Geoffrey. (2002) *Defining Language: A local grammar of definition sentences*. Amsterdam: John Benjamins Publishers.

Omrane, Walid., Bauwens, Luc., and Giot, Pierre. (2005) 'News Announcements, Market Activity and Volatility in the Euro/Dollar Foreign Exchange Market'. *Journal of International Money and Finance*, 24 (7), pp. 1108-1125.

Brill, Eric. (1993) 'Automatic Grammar Induction and Parsing Free Text: A transformation-based approach'. In *Proc. of 31th Annual Meeting of the Association for Computational Linguistics*, Ohio.

Chan, Wesley. (2003) 'Stock Price Reaction to News and No-News. Drift and Reversal after Headlines'. *Journal of Financial Economics*, 70(2), pp. 223-260.

Ciravegna, Fabio. and Wilks, Yorick. (2003) 'Designing Adaptive Information Extraction for the Semantic Web in Amilcare'. In (Eds.) Siegfried Handschuh and Steffen Staab, *Annotation for the Semantic Web, Frontiers in Artificial Intelligence and Applications*. US: IOS Press.

Cutler, David., Poterba, James., and Summers, Lawrence. (1989) 'What Moves Stock Prices?'. *Journal of Portfolio Management*, 15(3), pp. 4-12.

Debnath, Sandip. and Giles, C. Lee. (2005) 'A Learning Based Model for Headline Extraction of News Articles to Find Explanatory Sentences for Events'. In *Proc. of the 3rd international conference on Knowledge capture*, Alberta, Canada.

Engle, Robert. and K. Ng, Victor. (1993) 'Measuring and Testing the Impact of News on Volatility', *Journal of Finance*, 48(5), pp. 1749-1777.

Gao, Jianfeng., Li, Mu., Wu, Andi. and Huang, Chang-Ning (2005) 'Chinese Word Segmentation and Named Entity Recognition: A Pragmatic Approach', *Journal of Computational Linguistics*, 31(4), Cambridge, Mass.: MIT Press, pp. 531-574

Gross, Maurice. (1997) 'The Construction of Local Grammars'. In (Eds.) Roche, E. and Schabès, Y., *Finite-State Language Processing, Language, Speech, and Communication*, Cambridge, Mass.: MIT Press, pp. 329-354.

Habash, Nizar. and Rambow, Owen. (2005) 'Arabic Tokenization, Morphological Analysis, and Part-of-Speech Tagging in One Fell Swoop'. In *Proc. of the Conference of American Association for Computational Linguistics (ACL'05)*, Ann Arbour, MI.

Halliday, Michael, A. K. (1993) 'On the language of Physical Sciences'. In (Eds.) Halliday, Michael. and Martin, J. R., *Writing Science* pp. 54-68. London: The Falmer Press.

Hardie, Iain. and MacKenzie, Donaled. (2005) 'An Economy of Calculation: Agencement and Distributed Cognition in a Hedge Fund'. (Available at http://www.sps.ed.ac.uk/staff/An%20Economy%20of%20Calculation.pdf).

Harris, Zellig. (1991) *A Theory of Language and Information: A Mathematical Approach*. Oxford: Clarendon Press.

Kittredge, Richard. and Lehrberger, John. (1982) *Sublanguage: Studies of language in restricted semantic domains*. Berlin: Walter de Gruyter.

Koppel, Moshe and Shtrimberg, Itai. (2004) 'Good News or Bad News? Let the Market Decide'. In *AAAI Spring Symposium on Exploring Attitude and Affect in Text*, Palo Alto: AAAI Press, pp. 86-88.

Mackenzie, Donald. (2000). 'Fear in the Markets'. *London Review of Books,* 22(8), pp 31-32.

McLernon, Brian. and Kushmerick, Nicholas. (2006) 'Transductive Pattern Learning for Information Extraction'. In *Proc. of EACL 2006 Workshop on Adaptive Text Extraction and Mining*, Trento.

Seo, Young-Woo., Giampapa, Joseph. and Sycara, Katia. (2002) 'Text Classification for Intelligent Agent Portfolio Management'. In *Proc. of the 1st International Joint Conference on Autonomous Agents and Multi-Agent Systems*, pp. 802-803, Bologna.

Shiller, Robert. (2000) *Irrational Exuberance*. Princeton: Princeton University Press.

Sinclair, John McH. (1996) *Collins COBUILD Grammar Patterns 1: Verbs*. HarperCollins, Glasgow.

Smadja, Frank. (1994) 'Retrieving Collocations from Text: Xtract'. In (Eds.) Armstrong, S., *Using Large Corpora*. London: MIT Press.

Stevenson, Mark. and Greenwood, Mark A. (2005) 'A Semantic Approach to IE Pattern Induction'. In *Proc. of the 43rd Meeting of the Association for Computational Linguistics (ACL'05)*, pp. 379-386, Ann Arbour, MI.

Wilks, Yorick (1998) 'Inducing Adequate Grammars from Electronic Texts', EPSRC ROPA Grant GR/K/66215 Final Report. (Available at http://nlp.shef.ac.uk/research/reports/k66215.html).

Yangarber, Roman. (2003) 'Counter-Training in Discovery of Semantic Patterns'. In *Proc. of the 41st Annual Meeting of the Association for Computational Linguistics (ACL 2003)*, pp. 343-350, Sapporo, Japan.

Learning Domain-Specific Information Extraction Patterns from the Web

Siddharth Patwardhan and Ellen Riloff
School of Computing
University of Utah
Salt Lake City, UT 84112
{sidd,riloff}@cs.utah.edu

Abstract

Many information extraction (IE) systems rely on manually annotated training data to learn patterns or rules for extracting information about events. Manually annotating data is expensive, however, and a new data set must be annotated for each domain. So most IE training sets are relatively small. Consequently, IE patterns learned from annotated training sets often have limited coverage. In this paper, we explore the idea of using the Web to automatically identify domain-specific IE patterns that were not seen in the training data. We use IE patterns learned from the MUC-4 training set as anchors to identify domain-specific web pages and then learn new IE patterns from them. We compute the *semantic affinity* of each new pattern to automatically infer the type of information that it will extract. Experiments on the MUC-4 test set show that these new IE patterns improved recall with only a small precision loss.

1 Introduction

Information Extraction (IE) is the task of identifying event descriptions in natural language text and extracting information related to those events. Many IE systems use extraction patterns or rules to identify the relevant information (Soderland et al., 1995; Riloff, 1996; Califf and Mooney, 1999; Soderland, 1999; Yangarber et al., 2000). Most of these systems use annotated training data to learn pattern matching rules based on lexical, syntactic, and/or semantic information. The learned patterns are then used to locate relevant information in new texts.

IE systems typically focus on information about events that are relevant to a specific domain, such as terrorism (Sundheim, 1992; Soderland et al., 1995; Riloff, 1996; Chieu et al., 2003), management succession (Sundheim, 1995; Yangarber et al., 2000), or job announcements (Califf and Mooney, 1999; Freitag and McCallum, 2000). Supervised learning systems for IE depend on domain-specific training data, which consists of texts associated with the domain that have been manually annotated with event information.

The need for domain-specific training data has several disadvantages. Because of the manual labor involved in annotating a corpus, and because a new corpus must be annotated for each domain, most annotated IE corpora are relatively small. Language is so expressive that it is practically impossible for the patterns learned from a relatively small training set to cover all the different ways of describing events. Consequently, the IE patterns learned from manually annotated training sets typically represent only a subset of the IE patterns that could be useful for the task. Many recent approaches in natural language processing (Yarowsky, 1995; Collins and Singer, 1999; Riloff and Jones, 1999; Nigam et al., 2000; Wiebe and Riloff, 2005) have recognized the need to use unannotated data to improve performance.

While the Web provides a vast repository of unannotated texts, it is non-trivial to identify texts that belong to a particular domain. The difficulty is that web pages are not specifically annotated with tags categorizing their content. Nevertheless, in this paper we look to the Web as a vast dynamic resource for domain-specific IE learning. Our approach exploits an existing set of IE patterns that were learned from annotated training data to automatically identify new, domain-specific texts from

Proceedings of the Workshop on Information Extraction Beyond The Document, pages 66–73,
Sydney, July 2006.

the Web. These web pages are then used for additional IE training, yielding a new set of domain-specific IE patterns. Experiments on the MUC-4 test set show that the new IE patterns improve coverage for the domain.

This paper is organized as follows. Section 2 presents the MUC-4 IE task and data that we use in our experiments. Section 3 describes how we create a baseline IE system from the MUC-4 training data. Section 4 describes the collection and preprocessing of potentially relevant web pages. Section 5 then explains how we use the IE patterns learned from the MUC-4 training set as anchors to learn new IE patterns from the web pages. We also compute the *semantic affinity* of each new pattern to automatically infer the type of information that it will extract. Section 6 shows experimental results for two types of extractions, victims and targets, on the MUC-4 test set. Finally, Section 7 compares our approach to related research, and Section 8 concludes with ideas for future work.

2 The MUC-4 IE Task and Data

The focus of our research is on the MUC-4 information extraction task (Sundheim, 1992), which is to extract information about terrorist events. The MUC-4 corpus contains 1700 stories, mainly news articles related to Latin American terrorism, and associated *answer key templates* containing the information that should be extracted from each story.

We focused our efforts on two of the MUC-4 *string* slots, which require textual extractions: human targets (victims) and physical targets. The MUC-4 data has proven to be an especially difficult IE task for a variety of reasons, including the fact that the texts are entirely in upper case, roughly 50% of the texts are irrelevant (i.e., they do not describe a relevant terrorist event), and many of the stories that are relevant describe multiple terrorist events that need to be teased apart. The best results reported across all string slots in MUC-4 were in the 50%-70% range for recall and precision (Sundheim, 1992), with most of the MUC-4 systems relying on heavily hand-engineered components. Chieu et al. (2003) recently developed a fully automatic template generator for the MUC-4 IE task. Their best system produced recall scores of 41%-44% with precision scores of 49%-51% on the TST3 and TST4 test sets.

3 Learning IE Patterns from a Fixed Training Set

As our baseline system, we created an IE system for the MUC-4 terrorism domain using the AutoSlog-TS extraction pattern learning system (Riloff, 1996; Riloff and Phillips, 2004), which is freely available for research use. AutoSlog-TS is a weakly supervised learner that requires two sets of texts for training: texts that are relevant to the domain and texts that are irrelevant to the domain. The MUC-4 data includes relevance judgments (implicit in the answer keys), which we used to partition our training set into relevant and irrelevant subsets.

AutoSlog-TS' learning process has two phases. In the first phase, syntactic patterns are applied to the training corpus in an exhaustive fashion, so that extraction patterns are generated for (literally) every lexical instantiation of the patterns that appears in the corpus. For example, the syntactic pattern "*<subj> PassVP*" would generate extraction patterns for all verbs that appear in the corpus in a passive voice construction. The subject of the verb will be extracted. In the terrorism domain, some of these extraction patterns might be: "*<subj> PassVP(murdered)*" and "*<subj> PassVP(bombed).*" These would match sentences such as: "the mayor was murdered", and "the embassy and hotel were bombed". Figure 1 shows the 17 types of extraction patterns that AutoSlog-TS currently generates. PassVP refers to passive voice verb phrases (VPs), ActVP refers to active voice VPs, InfVP refers to infinitive VPs, and AuxVP refers to VPs where the main verb is a form of "to be" or "to have". Subjects (subj), direct objects (dobj), PP objects (np), and possessives can be extracted by the patterns.

In the second phase, AutoSlog-TS applies all of the generated extraction patterns to the training corpus and gathers statistics for how often each pattern occurs in relevant versus irrelevant texts. The extraction patterns are subsequently ranked based on their association with the domain, and then a person manually reviews the patterns, deciding which ones to keep[1] and assigning thematic roles to them. We manually defined selectional restrictions for each slot type (victim and target)

[1]Typically, many patterns are strongly associated with the domain but will not extract information that is relevant to the IE task. For example, in this work we only care about patterns that will extract victims and targets. Patterns that extract other types of information are not of interest.

Pattern Type	Example Pattern
<subj> PassVP	<victim> was murdered
<subj> ActVP	<perp> murdered
<subj> ActVP Dobj	<weapon> caused damage
<subj> ActInfVP	<perp> tried to kill
<subj> PassInfVP	<weapon> was intended to kill
<subj> AuxVP Dobj	<victim> was casualty
<subj> AuxVP Adj	<victim> is dead
ActVP <dobj>	bombed <target>
InfVP <dobj>	to kill <victim>
ActInfVP <dobj>	planned to bomb <target>
PassInfVP <dobj>	was planned to kill <victim>
Subj AuxVP <dobj>	fatality is <victim>
NP Prep <np>	attack against <target>
ActVP Prep <np>	killed with <weapon>
PassVP Prep <np>	was killed with <weapon>
InfVP Prep <np>	to destroy with <weapon>
<possessive> NP	<victim>'s murder

Figure 1: AutoSlog-TS' pattern types and sample IE patterns

and then automatically added these to each pattern when the role was assigned.

On our training set, AutoSlog-TS generated 40,553 distinct extraction patterns. A person manually reviewed all of the extraction patterns that had a score ≥ 0.951 and frequency ≥ 3. This score corresponds to AutoSlog-TS' RlogF metric, described in (Riloff, 1996). The lowest ranked patterns that passed our thresholds had at least 3 relevant extractions out of 5 total extractions. In all, 2,808 patterns passed the thresholds. The reviewer ultimately decided that 396 of the patterns were useful for the MUC-4 IE task, of which 291 were useful for extracting victims and targets.

4 Data Collection

In this research, our goal is to automatically learn IE patterns from a large, domain-independent text collection, such as the Web. The billions of freely available documents on the World Wide Web and its ever-growing size make the Web a potential source of data for many corpus-based natural language processing tasks. Indeed, many researchers have recently tapped the Web as a data-source for improving performance on NLP tasks (e.g., Resnik (1999), Ravichandran and Hovy (2002), Keller and Lapata (2003)). Despite these successes, numerous problems exist with collecting data from the Web, such as web pages containing information that is not free text, including advertisements, embedded scripts, tables, captions, etc. Also, the documents cover many genres, and it is not easy to identify documents of a particular genre or domain. Additionally, most of the documents are in HTML, and some amount of processing is required to extract the free text. In the following subsections we describe the process of collecting a corpus of terrorism-related CNN news articles from the Web.

4.1 Collecting Domain-Specific Texts

Our goal was to automatically identify and collect a set of documents that are similar in domain to the MUC-4 terrorism text collection. To create such a corpus, we used hand-crafted queries given to a search engine. The queries to the search engine were manually created to try to ensure that the majority of the documents returned by the search engine would be terrorism-related. Each query consisted of two parts: (1) the name of a terrorist organization, and (2) a word or phrase describing a terrorist action (such as *bombed*, *kidnapped*, etc.). The following lists of 5 terrorist organizations and 16 terrorist actions were used to create search engine queries:

Terrorist organizations: *Al Qaeda, ELN, FARC, HAMAS, IRA*

Terrorist actions: *assassinated, assassination, blew up, bombed, bombing, bombs, explosion, hijacked, hijacking, injured, kidnapped, kidnapping, killed, murder, suicide bomber, wounded.*

We created a total of 80 different queries representing each possible combination of a terrorist organization and a terrorist action.

We used the *Google*[2] search engine with the help of the freely available *Google API*[3] to locate the texts on the Web. To ensure that we retrieved only CNN news articles, we restricted the search to the domain "`cnn.com`" by adding the "`site:`" option to each of the queries. We also restricted the search to English language documents by initializing the API with the `lang_en` option. We deleted documents whose URLs contained the word "transcript" because most of these were transcriptions of CNN's TV shows and were stylistically very different from written text. We ran the 80 queries twice, once in December 2005 and once in April 2005, which produced 3,496 documents and 3,309 documents, respectively. After removing duplicate articles, we were left

[2]http://www.google.com

[3]http://www.google.com/apis

with a total of 6,182 potentially relevant terrorism articles.

4.2 Processing the Texts

The downloaded documents were all HTML documents containing HTML tags and JavaScript intermingled with the news text. The CNN webpages typically also contained advertisements, text for navigating the website, headlines and links to other stories. All of these things could be problematic for our information extraction system, which was designed to process narrative text using a shallow parser. Thus, simply deleting all HTML tags on the page would not have given us natural language sentences. Instead, we took advantage of the uniformity of the CNN web pages to "clean" them and extract just the sentences corresponding to the news story.

We used a tool called *HTMLParser*[4] to parse the HTML code, and then deleted all nodes in the HTML parse trees corresponding to tables, comments, and embedded scripts (such as JavaScript or VBScript). The system automatically extracted news text starting from the headline (embedded in an *H1* HTML element) and inferred the end of the article text using a set of textual clues such as *"Feedback:"*, *"Copyright 2005"*, *"contributed to this report"*, etc. In case of any ambiguity, all of the text on the web page was extracted.

The size of the text documents ranged from 0 bytes to 255 kilobytes. The empty documents were due to dead links that the search engine had indexed at an earlier time, but which no longer existed. Some extremely small documents also resulted from web pages that had virtually no free text on them, so only a few words remained after the HTML had been stripped. Consequently, we removed all documents less than 10 bytes in size. Upon inspection, we found that many of the largest documents were political articles, such as political party platforms and transcriptions of political speeches, which contained only brief references to terrorist events. To prevent the large documents from skewing the corpus, we also deleted all documents over 10 kilobytes in size. At the end of this process we were left with a CNN terrorism news corpus of 5,618 documents, each with an average size of about 648 words. In the rest of the paper we will refer to these texts as "the CNN terrorism web pages".

[4]http://htmlparser.sourceforge.net

5 Learning Domain-Specific IE Patterns from Web Pages

Having created a large domain-specific corpus from the Web, we are faced with the problem of identifying the useful extraction patterns from these new texts. Our basic approach is to use the patterns learned from the fixed training set as *seed patterns* to identify sentences in the CNN terrorism web pages that describe a terrorist event. We hypothesized that extraction patterns occurring in the same sentence as a seed pattern are likely to be associated with terrorism.

Our process for learning new domain-specific IE patterns has two phases, which are described in the following sections. Section 5.1 describes how we produce a ranked list of candidate extraction patterns from the CNN terrorism web pages. Section 5.2 explains how we filter these patterns based on the *semantic affinity* of their extractions, which is a measure of the tendency of the pattern to extract entities of a desired semantic category.

5.1 Identifying Candidate Patterns

The first goal was to identify extraction patterns that were relevant to our domain: terrorist events. We began by exhaustively generating every possible extraction pattern that occurred in our CNN terrorism web pages. We applied the AutoSlog-TS system (Riloff, 1996) to the web pages to automatically generate all lexical instantiations of patterns in the corpus. Collectively, the resulting patterns were capable of extracting every noun phrase in the CNN collection. In all, 147,712 unique extraction patterns were created as a result of this process.

Next, we computed the statistical correlation of each extraction pattern with the seed patterns based on the frequency of their occurrence in the same sentence. IE patterns that never occurred in the same sentence as a seed pattern were discarded. We used Pointwise Mutual Information (PMI) (Manning and Schütze, 1999; Banerjee and Pedersen, 2003) as the measure of statistical correlation. Intuitively, an extraction pattern that occurs more often than chance in the same sentence as a seed pattern will have a high PMI score.

The 147,712 extraction patterns acquired from the CNN terrorism web pages were then ranked by their PMI correlation to the seed patterns. Table 1 lists the most highly ranked patterns. Many of these patterns do seem to be related to terrorism,

<subj> killed sgt	<subj> destroyed factories
<subj> burned flag	explode after <np>
sympathizers of <np>	<subj> killed heir
<subj> kills bystanders	<subj> shattered roof
rescued within <np>	fled behind <np>

Table 1: Examples of candidate patterns that are highly correlated with the terrorism seed patterns

but many of them are not useful to our IE task (for this paper, identifying the victims and physical targets of a terrorist attack). For example, the pattern *"explode after <np>"* will not extract victims or physical targets, while the pattern *"sympathizers of <np>"* may extract people but they would not be the *victims* of an attack. In the next section, we explain how we filter and re-rank these candidate patterns to identify the ones that are directly useful to our IE task.

5.2 Filtering Patterns based upon their Semantic Affinity

Our next goal is to filter out the patterns that are not useful for our IE task, and to automatically assign the correct slot type (victim or target) to the ones that are relevant. To automatically determine the mapping between extractions and slots, we define a measure called *semantic affinity*. The semantic affinity of an extraction pattern to a semantic category is a measure of its tendency to extract NPs belonging to that semantic category. This measure serves two purposes:

(a) It allows us to filter out candidate patterns that do not have a strong semantic affinity to our categories of interest.

(b) It allows us to define a mapping between the extractions of the candidate patterns and the desired slot types.

We computed the semantic affinity of each candidate extraction pattern with respect to six semantic categories: *target*, *victim*, *perpetrator*, *organization*, *weapon* and *other*. Targets and victims are our categories of interest. Perpetrators, organizations, and weapons are common semantic classes in this domain which could be "distractors". The other category is a catch-all to represent all other semantic classes. To identify the semantic class of each noun phrase, we used the Sundance package (Riloff and Phillips, 2004), which is a freely available shallow parser that uses dictionaries to assign semantic classes to words and phrases.

We counted the frequencies of the semantic categories extracted by each candidate pattern and applied the RLogF measure used by AutoSlog-TS (Riloff, 1996) to rank the patterns based on their affinity for the target and victim semantic classes. For example, the semantic affinity of an extraction pattern for the target semantic class would be calculated as:

$$\text{affinity}_{pattern} = \frac{f_{target}}{f_{all}} \cdot \log_2 f_{target} \quad (1)$$

where f_{target} is the number of target semantic class extractions and $f_{all} = f_{target} + f_{victim} + f_{perp} + f_{org} + f_{weapon} + f_{other}$. This is essentially a probability $P(target)$ weighted by the log of the frequency.

We then used two criteria to remove patterns that are not strongly associated with a desired semantic category. If the semantic affinity of a pattern for category C was (1) greater than a threshold, and (2) greater than its affinity for the *other* category, then the pattern was deemed to have a semantic affinity for category C. Note that we intentionally allow for a pattern to have an affinity for more than one semantic category (except for the catch-all *other* class) because this is fairly common in practice. For example, the pattern *"attack on <np>"* frequently extracts both targets (e.g., *"an attack on the U.S. embassy"*) and victims (e.g., *"an attack on the mayor of Bogota"*). Our hope is that such a pattern would receive a high semantic affinity ranking for both categories.

Table 2 shows the top 10 high frequency ($freq \geq 50$) patterns that were judged to have a strong semantic affinity for the target and victim categories. There are clearly some incorrect entries (e.g., *"<subj> fired missiles"* is more likely to identify perpetrators than targets), but most of the patterns are indeed good extractors for the desired categories. For example, *"fired into <np>"*, *"went off in <np>"*, and *"car bomb near <np>"* are all good patterns for identifying targets of a terrorist attack. In general, the semantic affinity measure seemed to do a reasonably good job of filtering patterns that are not relevant to our task, and identifying patterns that are useful for extracting victims and targets.

6 Experiments and Results

Our goal has been to use IE patterns learned from a fixed, domain-specific training set to automatically learn additional IE patterns from a large,

Target Patterns	Victim Patterns
<subj> fired missiles	wounded in <np>
missiles at <np>	<subj> was identified
bomb near <np>	wounding <dobj>
fired into <np>	<subj> wounding
died on <np>	identified <dobj>
went off in <np>	<subj> identified
car bomb near <np>	including <dobj>
exploded outside <np>	<subj> ahmed
gunmen on <np>	<subj> lying
killed near <np>	<subj> including

Table 2: Top 10 high-frequency target and victim patterns learned from the Web

domain-independent text collection, such as the Web. Although many of the patterns learned from the CNN terrorism web pages look like good extractors, an open question was whether they would actually be useful for the original IE task. For example, some of the patterns learned from the CNN web pages have to do with beheadings (e.g., *"beheading of <np>"* and *"beheaded <np>"*), which are undeniably good victim extractors. But the MUC-4 corpus primarily concerns Latin American terrorism that does not involve beheading incidents. In general, the question is whether IE patterns learned from a large, diverse text collection can be valuable for a specific IE task above and beyond the patterns that were learned from the domain-specific training set, or whether the newly learned patterns will simply not be applicable. To answer this question, we evaluated the newly learned IE patterns on the MUC-4 test set.

The MUC-4 data set is divided into 1300 development (DEV) texts, and four test sets of 100 texts each (TST1, TST2, TST3, and TST4).[5] All of these texts have associated answer key templates. We used 1500 texts (DEV+TST1+TST2) as our training set, and 200 texts (TST3+TST4) as our test set.

The IE process typically involves extracting information from individual sentences and then mapping that information into answer key templates, one template for each terrorist event described in the story. The process of template generation requires discourse processing to determine how many events took place and which facts correspond to which event. Discourse processing and template generation are not the focus of this paper. Our research aims to produce a larger set of extraction patterns so that more information will be extracted from the sentences, before discourse analysis would begin. Consequently, we evaluate the performance of our IE system at that stage: after extracting information from sentences, but before template generation takes place. This approach directly measures how well we are able to improve the coverage of our extraction patterns for the domain.

6.1 Baseline Results on the MUC-4 IE Task

The AutoSlog-TS system described in Section 3 used the MUC-4 training set to learn 291 target and victim IE patterns. These patterns produced 64% recall with 43% precision on the targets, and 50% recall with 52% precision on the victims.[6]

These numbers are not directly comparable to the official MUC-4 scores, which evaluate template generation, but our recall is in the same ballpark. Our precision is lower, but this is to be expected because we do not perform discourse analysis.[7] These 291 IE patterns represent our *baseline* IE system that was created from the MUC-4 training data.

6.2 Evaluating the Newly Learned Patterns

We used all 396 terrorism extraction patterns learned from the MUC-4 training set[8] as seeds to identify relevant text regions in the CNN terrorism web pages. We then produced a ranked list of new terrorism IE patterns using a semantic affinity cutoff of 3.0. We selected the top N patterns from the ranked list, with N ranging from 50 to 300, and added these N patterns to the baseline system.

Table 3 lists the recall, precision and F-measure for the increasingly larger pattern sets. For the tar-

[5]The DEV texts were used for development in MUC-3 and MUC-4. The TST1 and TST2 texts were used as test sets for MUC-3 and then as development texts for MUC-4. The TST3 and TST4 texts were used as the test sets for MUC-4.

[6]We used a *head noun* scoring scheme, where we scored an extraction as correct if its head noun matched the head noun in the answer key. This approach allows for different leading modifiers in an NP as long as the head noun is the same. For example, "armed men" will successfully match "5 armed men". We also discarded pronouns (they were not scored at all) because our system does not perform coreference resolution.

[7]Among other things, discourse processing merges seemingly disparate extractions based on coreference resolution (e.g., "the guerrillas" may refer to the same people as "the armed men") and applies task-specific constraints (e.g., the MUC-4 task definition has detailed rules about exactly what types of people are considered to be terrorists).

[8]This included not only the 291 target and victim patterns, but also 105 patterns associated with other types of terrorism information.

	Targets			Victims		
	Precision	Recall	F-measure	Precision	Recall	F-measure
baseline	0.425	0.642	0.511	0.498	0.517	0.507
50+baseline	0.420	0.642	0.508	0.498	0.517	0.507
100+baseline	0.419	0.650	0.510	0.496	0.521	0.508
150+baseline	0.415	0.650	0.507	0.480	0.521	0.500
200+baseline	0.412	0.667	0.509	0.478	0.521	0.499
250+baseline	0.401	0.691	0.507	0.478	0.521	0.499
300+baseline	0.394	0.691	0.502	0.471	0.542	0.504

Table 3: Performance of new IE patterns on MUC-4 test set

get slot, the recall increases from 64.2% to 69.1% with a small drop in precision. The F-measure drops by about 1% because recall and precision are less balanced. But we gain more in recall (+5%) than we lose in precision (-3%). For the victim patterns, the recall increases from 51.7% to 54.2% with a similar small drop in precision. The overall drop in the F-measure in this case is negligible. These results show that our approach for learning IE patterns from a large, diverse text collection (the Web) can indeed improve coverage on a domain-specific IE task, with a small decrease in precision.

7 Related Work

Unannotated texts have been used successfully for a variety of NLP tasks, including named entity recognition (Collins and Singer, 1999), subjectivity classification (Wiebe and Riloff, 2005), text classification (Nigam et al., 2000), and word sense disambiguation (Yarowsky, 1995). The Web has become a popular choice as a resource for large quantities of unannotated data. Many research ideas have exploited the Web in unsupervised or weakly supervised algorithms for natural language processing (e.g., Resnik (1999), Ravichandran and Hovy (2002), Keller and Lapata (2003)).

The use of unannotated data to improve information extraction is not new. Unannotated texts have been used for weakly supervised training of IE systems (Riloff, 1996) and in bootstrapping methods that begin with seed words or patterns (Riloff and Jones, 1999; Yangarber et al., 2000). However, those previous systems rely on pre-existing domain-specific corpora. For example, EXDISCO (Yangarber et al., 2000) used Wall Street Journal articles for training. AutoSlog-TS (Riloff, 1996) and Meta-bootstrapping (Riloff and Jones, 1999) used the MUC-4 training texts. Meta-bootstrapping was also trained on web pages, but the "domain" was corporate relationships so domain-specific web pages were easily identified simply by gathering corporate web pages.

The KNOWITALL system (Popescu et al., 2004) also uses unannotated web pages for information extraction. However, this work is quite different from ours because KNOWITALL focuses on extracting domain-independent relationships with the aim of extending an ontology. In contrast, our work focuses on using the Web to augment a domain-specific, event-oriented IE system with new, automatically generated domain-specific IE patterns acquired from the Web.

8 Conclusions and Future Work

We have shown that it is possible to learn new extraction patterns for a domain-specific IE task by automatically identifying domain-specific web pages using seed patterns. Our approach produced a 5% increase in recall for extracting targets and a 3% increase in recall for extracting victims of terrorist events. Both increases in recall were at the cost of a small loss in precision.

In future work, we plan to develop improved ranking methods and more sophisticated semantic affinity measures to further improve coverage and minimize precision loss. Another possible avenue for future work is to embed this approach in a bootstrapping mechanism so that the most reliable new IE patterns can be used to collect additional web pages, which can then be used to learn more IE patterns in an iterative fashion. Also, while most of this process is automated, some human intervention is required to create the search queries for the document collection process, and to generate the seed patterns. We plan to look into techniques to automate these manual tasks as well.

Acknowledgments

This research was supported by NSF Grant IIS-0208985 and the Institute for Scientific Computing Research and the Center for Applied Scientific Computing within Lawrence Livermore National Laboratory.

References

S. Banerjee and T. Pedersen. 2003. The Design, Implementation, and Use of the Ngram Statistics Package. In *Proceedings of the Fourth International Conference on Intelligent Text Processing and Computational Linguistics*, pages 370–381, Mexico City, Mexico, February.

M. Califf and R. Mooney. 1999. Relational Learning of Pattern-matching Rules for Information Extraction. In *Proceedings of the Sixteenth National Conference on Artificial Intelligence*, pages 328–334, Orlando, FL, July.

H. Chieu, H. Ng, and Y. Lee. 2003. Closing the Gap: Learning-Based Information Extraction Rivaling Knowledge-Engineering Methods. In *Proceedings of the 41st Annual Meeting of the Association for Computational Linguistics*, pages 216–223, Sapporo, Japan, July.

M. Collins and Y. Singer. 1999. Unsupervised Models for Named Entity Classification. In *Proceedings of Joint SIGDAT Conference on Empirical Methods in Natural Language Processing and Very Large Corpora*, pages 100–110, College Park, MD, June.

D. Freitag and A. McCallum. 2000. Information Extraction with HMM Structures Learned by Stochastic Optimization. In *Proceedings of the Seventeenth National Conference on Artificial Intelligence*, pages 584–589, Austin, TX, August.

F. Keller and M. Lapata. 2003. Using the Web to Obtain Frequencies for Unseen Bigrams. *Computational Linguistics*, 29(3):459–484, September.

C. Manning and H. Schütze. 1999. *Foundations of Statistical Natural Language Processing*. The MIT Press, Cambridge, MA.

K. Nigam, A. McCallum, S. Thrun, and T. Mitchell. 2000. Text Classification from Labeled and Unlabeled Documents using EM. *Machine Learning*, 39(2-3):103–134, May.

A. Popescu, A. Yates, and O. Etzioni. 2004. Class Extraction from the World Wide Web. In Ion Muslea, editor, *Adaptive Text Extraction and Mining: Papers from the 2004 AAAI Workshop*, pages 68–73, San Jose, CA, July.

D. Ravichandran and E. Hovy. 2002. Learning Surface Text Patterns for a Question Answering System. In *Proceedings of the 40th Annual Meeting on Association for Computational Linguistics*, pages 41–47, Philadelphia, PA, July.

P. Resnik. 1999. Mining the Web for Bilingual Text. In *Proceedings of the 37th meeting of the Association for Computational Linguistics*, pages 527–534, College Park, MD, June.

E. Riloff and R. Jones. 1999. Learning Dictionaries for Information Extraction by Multi-Level Bootstrapping. In *Proceedings of the Sixteenth National Conference on Artificial Intelligence*, pages 474–479, Orlando, FL, July.

E. Riloff and W. Phillips. 2004. An Introduction to the Sundance and AutoSlog Systems. Technical Report UUCS-04-015, School of Computing, University of Utah.

E. Riloff. 1996. Automatically Generating Extraction Patterns from Untagged Text. In *Proceedings of the Thirteenth National Conference on Articial Intelligence*, pages 1044–1049, Portland, OR, August.

S. Soderland, D. Fisher, J. Aseltine, and W. Lehnert. 1995. CRYSTAL: Inducing a Conceptual Dictionary. In *Proceedings of the Fourteenth International Joint Conference on Artificial Intelligence*, pages 1314–1319, Montreal, Canada, August.

S. Soderland. 1999. Learning Information Extraction Rules for Semi-Structured and Free Text. *Machine Learning*, 34(1-3):233–272, February.

B. Sundheim. 1992. Overview of the Fourth Message Understanding Evaluation and Conference. In *Proceedings of the Fourth Message Understanding Conference (MUC-4)*, pages 3–21, McLean, VA, June.

B. Sundheim. 1995. Overview of the Results of the MUC-6 Evaluation. In *Proceedings of the Sixth Message Understanding Conference (MUC-6)*, pages 13–31, Columbia, MD, November.

J. Wiebe and E. Riloff. 2005. Creating Subjective and Objective Sentence Classifiers from Unannotated Texts. In *Proceedings of the 6th International Conference on Computational Linguistics and Intelligent Text Processing*, pages 486–497, Mexico City, Mexico, February.

R. Yangarber, R. Grishman, P. Tapanainen, and S. Huttunen. 2000. Automatic Acquisition of Domain Knowledge for Information Extraction. In *Proceedings of the 18th International Conference on Computational Linguistics*, pages 940–946, Saarbrücken, Germany, August.

D. Yarowsky. 1995. Unsupervised Word Sense Disambiguation Rivaling Supervised Methods. In *Proceedings of the 33rd Annual Meeting of the Association for Computational Linguistics*, pages 189–196, Cambridge, MA, June.

Author Index

Association for Computational Linguistics
209 N. Eighth Street
Stroudsburg, Pennsylvania 18360